MW00565005

Critical Storytelling

Critical Storytelling

VOLUME 5

The titles published in this series are listed at *brill.com/csto*

Critical Storytelling

Multilingual Immigrants in the United States

Edited by

Luis Javier Pentón Herrera and Ethan Tính Trịnh

BRILL
SENSE

LEIDEN | BOSTON

All chapters in this book have undergone peer review.

The Library of Congress Cataloging-in-Publication Data is available online at http://catalog.loc.gov

Typeface for the Latin, Greek, and Cyrillic scripts: "Brill". See and download: brill.com/brill-typeface.

ISSN 2590-0099
ISBN 978-90-04-42604-7 (paperback)
ISBN 978-90-04-42605-4 (hardback)
ISBN 978-90-04-44618-2 (e-book)

This book is printed on acid-free paper and produced in a sustainable manner.

Este libro está dedicado a toda mi familia y, en especial, a mis padres, Diana de los Santos Herrera Machín y Juan J. Pentón Uz. Gracias por su amor y guía durante toda mi vida. Hoy día soy quien soy gracias a ustedes.

This book is dedicated to my family and, especially, to my parents, Diana de los Santos Herrera Machín and Juan J. Pentón Uz. Thank you for your love and guidance throughout my life. Today I am who I am thanks to you.
— LUIS JAVIER PENTÓN HERRERA

• • •

Cuốn sách này là lời cảm ơn dành cho gia đình: Đức Trịnh, Phượng Phùng, Tuấn Trịnh. Cảm ơn mọi người vì những câu chuyện trong mỗi buổi ăn đã giúp con viết cuốn sách này. Cảm ơn sự hy sinh của Cha Mẹ dành cho con. Con xin chân thành cảm ơn.

This book is dedicated to my family, Đức Trịnh, Phượng Phùng, and Tuấn Trịnh. Thank you for the mundane stories in our meals that fed me with critical thinking during this project. Thank you for your sacrifice to make me who I am today. Thank you.
— ETHAN TÍNH TRỊNH

Contents

PART 2
PERSONAL NARRATIVES

Foreword

Gloria Park

Engaging in Critical Storytelling as a Transnational Immigrant Woman in Academy: (Un)Learning from Our Stories and Lived Experiences

The poems, personal narratives, and visual narratives penned in this edited volume are symbolic of human agency and resilience. These symbolic narratives provide readers additional hope and courage to transcend challenging life experiences into something that is victorious and transformative. These narratives, while authored by different individuals, are shared by all of us as we shuttle between nations, languages, families, races, genders, classes, ethnicities, and alike to renegotiate and (de)/(re)construct our identities and places in ever-changing social worlds. The voices in the chapters challenge the normative structures in order to position themselves as rightfully endowed members of multiple worlds. These voices carry with them refreshing perspectives in articulating what it means to write for publication in academia, and problematize the troubling ideology of who is educated and who has the right to shuttle between Englishes and our native languages.

The voices in these chapters bellow a powerful reminder for me that the very place to educate and transform individuals can be a source of isolation, (self)-marginalization, and powerlessness. I often feel isolated because my own words, voices, and experiences are closeted and do not align with the experiences and voices of the dominant images pervasive in the educational sector. A sense of (self)-marginalization prevails over my critical identity as a transnational, immigrant woman who shuttles between languages, and is compelled to write for the academic community that privileges certain discourses and norms. Equally important is a sense of powerlessness that often comes with not being able to champion the teachers, scholars, and authors from the peripheral contexts. Writing for publication can be so foreign to many of us who desire to tell our stories and share our lived experiences.

My reading of these chapters brought back memories of (1) immigrating to the U.S. in the late 1970s, (2) being in English-only classes from the late 1970s to the 1980s with peers who do not share my language, my culture, and my race, and (3) witnessing my parents working day and night to provide for us to constantly reach for the so-called "American Dream." I am reliving some of my lived experiences as a transnational woman shuttling between two linguistic and cultural worlds. I am once again called to reflect on how the chapters in this edited volume triggered similar memories of being and living in this country that is so familiar, yet foreign even after four decades.

In the rest of this introduction, I share a brief summary of each chapter in the *Poems* section. I also reflect on my lived experience with those of the authors' as a way to connect our shared stories of isolation, (self)-marginalization, powerlessness, yet privilege and transformation. In a similar manner, for the *Personal Narratives* section, I share a snapshot of the chapter summaries, then I discuss some emerging themes from the personal narratives and juxtapose my own personal stories in conversation with the themes. My personal stories, or my response to the authored chapters are aligned with Clandinin and Connelly's (2000) concept of temporality, weaving my stories back and forth, shuttling between past and present to inform my future as a transnational immigrant woman in academia. In the final section of this foreword (*Visual Narratives*), I privilege the chapters to speak for themselves and share a brief summary of each chapter. In closing this foreword, I share some critical questions as we continue to raise critical consciousness around finding a place to advance critical storytelling in both our personal and academic lives.

Poems

This section brings together nine (9) chapters of poetry work. I organized the poetry chapters into three thematic areas: (1) naming, erasure, and reclaiming identity, (2) pursuit of "American Dream," education, and professional identity, and (3) crossing borders of self and place. In addition to the grouped summary under each theme, I share my own stories that have been triggered by the authors' poetry rendition.

Critical Storytelling: Naming, Erasure, and Reclaiming Identity
The chapters by Lydiah Kananu Kiramba (Chapter 1) and Gabriel Teodoro Acevedo Velázquez (Chapter 3) are poems that discuss the importance of our native names, that are first bestowed on us at birth. The chapters point out that mispronouncing and shortening the names without consent becomes an unintentional erasure of the individual's ethnic, historical, and personal identities. Moreover, these "erasure" acts are often practiced by those in place of power, "whitewashing" names from diverse backgrounds to make it easier for them to pronounce.

I remember the first day (April 1976) of school in the U.S., all the teachers started to mispronounce my Korean name—Gui Sun "ghi" was botched to "guy," "gee." Of course, my immediate thought without being able to articulate my responses was that my Korean name was indeed difficult for my American teachers to pro-

nounce. I started to resent my parents for giving me such a difficult name. It was only until I got to middle school that I was able to help my teachers correctly pronounce my Korean name, which was on all my school records, and responded to my teachers, "you can call me Gloria!" Even with the act of "righting" my Korean name, I guess I felt ashamed of my Korean name, so I shared with my teachers my English given name. This new English name was given to me by one of my relatives who has been residing in the U.S. for a very long time. Keeping my Christian, Western name, perhaps, could be an act of assimilation or new birth. These chapters have triggered my memories of early school days when my embarrassment and shame surfaced due to others' mispronouncing of my Korean name. Thirty years later, I came back to the notion of naming and how my identities as a married woman with a biracial son have influenced my decision to keep my maiden last name, but my husband and I decided to provide Aidan with both Korean and Irish last name, not to lose his Korean and Irish heritage.

Critical Storytelling: Pursuit of "American" Dream, Education, and Professional Identity

The chapters by Sharada Krishnamurthy (Chapter 4), Manuel De Jesús Gómez Portillo (Chapter 5), and Ana Bautista (Chapter 6) illustrate the ways in which authors navigated and negotiated different spaces as immigrants fighting for their rights living the life of hope and courage, advocating for their children's (especially first-generation college attendees in the family) educational pursuit, and finding the paths toward reclaiming professional identity (returning to being a classroom teacher).

While I may not remember much about my need to pursue my dream, education, or even a career since my family and I immigrated to the U.S. in 1976 when I was 8 years old. What I do remember is my parents and my mother's extended family (who had already settled in the U.S. when we came to the U.S.) working for small restaurants and mechanic shops that were distant from what they used to do in Korea. Their career trajectory shifted dramatically due to the language and cultural barriers. My parents and my aunts/uncles were willing to start fresh, make a living, and live out their "American" dreams to put education first for their young children. The details of my family's immigrant journey are out of the scope of this Introduction. However, it is important to note that they, too, have navigated and negotiated challenging spaces to find a comfortable place for themselves and their children. Now that I reflect on the stories of Sharada, Manuel, and Ana, my parents sacrificed their lives to give "better" futures to their children.

Critical Storytelling: Crossing Borders of Self and Place

The chapters penned by R. Joseph Rodríguez (Chapter 2), Mauricio Patrón Rivera (Chapter 7), Zurisaray Espinosa (Chapter 8), and Jamie Harris (Chapter 9)

invite readers to promote change and hope in response to a sense of urgency
to act quickly but judiciously in a new locale. In that, these chapters document places of being and belonging as authors traverse cultures and languages
to remain transnational while physically planted in one locale. In particular,
Mauricio points out the places that shape our identity of being and becoming, and the relationships that are formed as a result of being in these places.
Zurisaray's Cuban identity had been erased from who she was for a very long
time until she mustered up the courage that allowed her to fight the battle to
voice her experiences. Jamie's rendition of her favorite Bible verse brings her
back to her Trinidadian roots and navigating those cultural practices that have
been dormant while living her life as a hyphenated individual, Trinidadian-
American.

   *When I was in high school, I always wondered why my parents were so into
Korean dramas, renting 10–15 VHS (video home system) tapes to watch in one sitting. Back in those days, the Korean videos were housed and rented out from large
Korean grocery stores (i.e., Lotte, H-Mart, etc). We are living in the U.S., and it's
not like we can go and visit whenever we want to, so why bother watching these
videos since they would only make my parents sad and homesick. It was only after
I was in college that I finally understood their desire to continue watching the
Korean dramas. I began watching Korean drama whenever I came home for the
summer from college. I got roped into my parents' after-work past time. I came to
understand the ways in which I was living in and moving in and out of, shuttling
between my Korean home (via Korean drama) and my reality in the U.S. Watching the Korean dramas gave me a sense of emotionally shuttling between Korea
and the U.S. Through watching these Korean dramas, I can live in the moment
of different characters, troubling events, and places of powerful relationships,
and I can forgive my parents for leaving the country where we feel belonged and
wanted. While I do not need to visit the Korean grocery store to rent the Korean
drama nowadays, I am privileged to continue to watch Korean dramas via Netflix.
Echoing Jamie's personal narrative, I can continue to embrace my transnational
and transcultural spaces as a hyphenated individual, living both as Korean and
naturalized U.S. citizen.*

Personal Narratives

In this section, there are 15 chapters. I share a brief summary of each authored
chapter, then I discuss the themes emerging from the authors' personal narratives. Following this, I juxtapose my own personal narratives in conversation with the themes: *Being and Belonging in Socially (Dis)Connected Worlds*;
Navigating Challenging yet Empowering Relationships; and *Advocating for and*

Transforming Self and Others. These themes can travel along a linear timeline, but they can also be iterative and circular, traveling back and forth between present and past to (re)imagine the future.

Critical Storytelling: Being and Belonging in the Socially (Dis)Connected Worlds

Babak Khoshnevisan's "Every Word Is True: An Autoethnography to Unravel My Story" is a powerful rendition of an Iranian finding a niche in the U.S. academic and cultural worlds. The uphill battles throughout the political, war-torn, and cultural challenges brought him more strengths and resilience.

Ethan Tính Trịnh's "Quê Hương" is an attempt by the author to illustrate the powerful political act of translating a deep, meaningful word, Quê Hương, into a concept, image, that only a transnational individual can begin to understand. The author's rendition of the translation process is an embodiment of their ever-fluid identities as a hyphenated scholar shuttling between and moving the cultural, linguistic, and academic worlds, and learning that led to "unlearning" of many areas.

Sandy Tadeo's "Pagbabalik: Does It Even Matter?" is an exploration of the author's (like many others like him) (un)fortunate realization regarding his linguistic capital and choices as he shuttles between finding himself in multiple social worlds. The challenges he took to be more fluent and be more accepted in the immigrant spaces provided him with the needed educational affordances.

Luis Javier Pentón Herrera's "My Life's Metamorphosis: Becoming Bilingual" is a narrative of believing in oneself as the author navigated different hills, mountains, and valleys in his immigrant journey—enlisting in the U.S. military, obtaining three Masters degrees, and coming to a full stop with a terminal degree of a Ph.D. Through the author's narrative, we come to understand how our linguistic choices and affordances take us far in life no matter how distant we may be from our heritage and/or additional languages. We always find our way back home.

Gloria Park: *In this part, I have the privilege of reflecting on my process of being, becoming, and belonging in my socially (dis)connected worlds. The powerful stories by these authors have triggered my journey navigating the challenging educational contexts to become a legitimate teacher-scholar and belong in the U.S. academia. Reading the above four chapters brought back some stories that have fueled my desire, commitment, and investment in continuing with my education. There were so many moments when I was ready to give up due to forces that were perceived to be stronger crushing down on me. You see, to these certain individuals, I simply could not be good enough to journey through a terminal degree—Ph.D. In the eyes of those individuals, I simply did not belong in their ver-*

sion of the academic community. However, there were others that saw me through a different set of lens and guided me with powerful words of wisdom. Now that I reflect on this process of being and becoming, both groups of people taught me a great deal about myself as a teacher-scholar, a transnational immigrant woman in academia, and a mother and spouse. Through these groups of individuals who privileged me in certain ways or marginalized in other ways, I found my super-hero inner strength to be mentored by trustworthy allies and to keep my enemies closer in order to reach my academic apex.

Critical Storytelling: Navigating Challenging yet Empowering Relationships

Ben Haseen's "Subtle Bangla Traits" is a powerful illustration of three siblings (un)learning of two worlds and how they negotiated their identities betwixt by those identities embraced and assigned by them and others. It is also about how the author's first teacher in the U.S.—Mr. Gutierrez—provided both space and awareness for him to develop as a young immigrant child in the U.S. public school system.

Pablo Montes' "Entre La Tierra Y Los Sueños" chronicles an intergeneration-al family story of honor, legacy, and knowledge that contradicts the normative discourses often embraced by the U.S.-based ideology of schooling and educa-tion. More importantly, the author's narrative is a true rendition of not losing oneself and family legacy as transnationals navigating to find one's dream and hope.

Bashar Al Hariri and Fatmeh Alalawneh's "Lost and Found: A Story of Re-claiming Identities" reminds us once again of the inner power and privilege that comes with upholding and embracing our ever-changing identities to en-act changes around social justice and transformation. Their collective stories provide us with evocative space to do more work around diversity, inclusivity, and social justice to look beyond accent and race.

Gloria Park: *In Critical Storytelling: Navigating Challenging yet Empowering Relationships section, I am reminded of multiple relationships that I have en-gaged in to be who I am today. There are so many individuals that have mentored me, knocked me down, and cared for me to be who I am today. Just as the personal narratives of Ben, Pablo, Bashar, and Fatmeh reveal, relationships, whether they are perceived as advantageous or not, become a critical medium in navigating difficult landscapes. The fact that my parents and my mother's extended family immigrated to the U.S. starting in the late 1960s to late 1970s was the starting point for how I situated myself in the world around me. My parents, especially my Mom, became a key player in my turbulent journey in the U.S. starting from 1976. You see, she took me out of a safe zone to nurture me, educate, and help me develop into the person I am today. With the help of my husband, I am hopeful that I can do the same for our son. Similarly, I also see myself as an academic mother to my dissertation advisees as well as those who reach out to me as a trusted mentor. My hope is that I can continue to build an empowering relationship with my dear Son and my academic children now and in the future.*

Critical Storytelling: Advocating for and Transforming Self and Others

Jiyoon Lee's "You Had Better Turn off the Fan..." is a rendition of bridging theory and practice—how a specified lived experience using English for the first time in the U.S. educational contexts and what that means for understanding and exploring communicative competence in learning and teaching English as an international language. This incident that occurred in 1999 has become a pedagogical tool for the author and her pre-service teacher education students.

Aracelis Nieves's "Como Una Leona: Shielding My Son from Discrimination at School" is a narrative rendition of one mother's journey as her son's advocate. These discriminations experienced by Diego, the author's son, were both intentional and unintentional ones, and voicing one's insights and experiences is the way to "right" the wrong and raise critical consciousness around those very issues.

May F. Chung's "I Lost My Language but Your Child Doesn't Have to..." explores the author's coming to terms with what it means to be a bilingual and bicultural individual and challenges of losing one's heritage language. Due to her lived experience, she has come to champion immigrant children's journeys in maintaining their heritage languages. Her narrative is close to home for many intergenerational immigrants shuttling between two very different languages and everything that comes with those languages.

Geovanny Vicente Romero's "Giving back When Most in Need" is a narrative of learning and teaching one's heritage (Spanish) and additional (English) languages as a stepping stone into his professional career trajectory. The author's narrative gets at the heart of what many immigrants experience—leaving their lucrative and high-status professions in their home countries and beginning blue-collared work due to linguistic hegemony and lack of choices in the U.S.

Gloria Park: *In the section of Critical Storytelling: Advocating for and Transforming Self and Others, I am reminded of the ways in which I came to be a teacher, scholar, mother, spouse, and peer. While these identities are overlapping at times and in conflict with one another, I can confidently state that these identities have (dis)empowered me and others throughout my journey. My lived experience as a transnational immigrant woman has always dictated what I bring into my classroom and how I navigate my teaching space as a critical pedagogue. Simply, myself and my life have been a constant resource in my pedagogy.*

Visual Narratives

There are four (4) chapters in this section. I share a brief summary of each chapter. The author(s) of each chapter powerfully weaves in the photos representing the themes.

Visual Storytelling: Weaving the Personal and the Political
Rajwan Alshareefy and Cristina Sánchez-Martín's "Journeying through Transnational Spaces: A Reflexive Account of Praxis and Identity Construction" is a powerful rendition of two teacher-scholars' coming together as a mentor and mentee in academia. Each author weaves a critical image that is at the center of his/her reflexive account. Their narratives depict a path of convergence and divergence where individual identities, while fluid and conflicted, are being challenged by societal level discourses that continue to marginalize and disrupt their individual and political choices. More critically, their narratives champion reflexive processes of coming to know oneself in order to advocate for those in similar, yet different terrains of transnational spaces.

Tairan Qiu's "The Weight of a Name: My Names and Stories across Lands and Time" illustrate autobiographical snapshots accompanied by photos of her development from a toddler to a married woman. These focus on the power that comes with naming in Chinese culture, as it is true in many cultures around the world. While her narrative concludes with a call for those from diverse linguistic and cultural backgrounds to move away from assimilation to the dominant cultures and images, it is critical for all of us to be mindful that not everyone is afforded the choice of navigating between embraced and assigned identities.

Judith Landeros' "Story Weaving: Tejidos de Conocimientos Que Nos Conectan al Territorio" is a powerful rendition of unpacking the hidden curriculum of our educational system. Specifically, her illustration of the narratives coupled with the photos portray the relationship between her maternal figure and the surrounding ecology, namely the plants, the water, and the Land. The author once again reminds us the power that comes with intergenerational, transnational, and translingual stories that are missing in our curriculum that continues to privilege and champion the White privilege and "American Dream" when so much of what is being curricularized in the public education is disconnected to who we are, what we do, and how we live.

Polina Vinogradova's "The Power of Digital Storytelling for English Language Education: A Reflective Essay" weaves together a personally and politically empowered narrative of one's educational journey as she wrestled through challenging terrain of literacy socialization and development to find peace with digital storytelling as an empowering pedagogical tool for herself and her students. The author situates her work by exposing the political nature of how reading and writing are taught in our educational landscape, and by providing a multimodal focus of learning to read and write, the teachers are provided with a platform to continue to make education inclusive of all.

Critical Storytelling: Moving Forward

It has been both my privilege and honor to read through these chapters. I learned much about the stories and the experiences of each author. I am grateful for this opportunity. I am once again reminded that our work, our voices, and our experiences should not end here with the publication of this edited volume. We must continue to do work in this area as teachers, scholars, teacher-scholars, educators, parents, and administrators alike to move forward to raise critical consciousness around issues of equity and access in our personal and professional lives. I leave you with these questions and I welcome additional questions of pedagogy, scholarship, and policy areas that we need to continue to wrestle with to make this world a better and more inclusive place.

- In what ways can we assist classroom teachers (as well as pre-service teachers) to bring authentic stories into their classrooms, not only in what and how they teach, but also as part of the classroom space?
- How can we re-conceptualize the K-20 curricula to include critical storytelling as a major theme that weaves across all curricula and not just an add-on course or special topic?
- How do we continue to promote the problem posing education that Paulo Freire (1970) envisioned for educators in the *Pedagogy of the Oppressed*?
- In what ways can the administrators of K-20 educational contexts be more involved in the day-to-day work of classroom teachers?
- How can journal editors continue to nurture, mentor, and work with authors and writers from around the globe, especially those who need direct mentorship of learning to write for publication?

References

Clandinin, D. J., & Connelly, F. M. (2000). *Narrative inquiry: Experience and story in qualitative research.* Jossey-Bass.

Freire, P. (1970). *Pedagogy of the oppressed.* Continuum.

Preface

The original idea for this edited volume first emerged back in late 2018/early 2019 when I, Luis, was teaching English to speakers of other languages (ESOL) to high school students in Maryland. After being rejected by two publishing houses, I reflected on the book proposal and I thought that perhaps it was not the right time to continue pursuing potential publishers. For this reason, I decided to give up on this idea and just left the draft on my desktop for a few months. Thankfully, I talked to Ethan one day about my vision for this edited volume as we worked on another project, and, with their support and encouragement, we combined forces and reached out to the series editors of Critical Storytelling, Nicholas and Brandon, who accepted our edited book proposal.

I, Ethan, am thankful that Luis invited me to work with him on this special project. When I was teaching ESOL to immigrant, transnational college students in Georgia, our class was discussing the topics of cultural differences, heritage appreciation, struggles, and successes of immigrants in the United States. During this time, I struggled to find relevant textbooks that we could use in our classroom to connect to our real-life experiences. The ESOL textbooks we currently use in our program teach grammar, writing and reading skills, but do not touch deeply on the social issues that transnational immigrants often face, such as language discrimination, gender identities, cultural negotiation, and family struggles, to name a few. I remember that after we finished a lesson where we explored the topic of the melting pot, a student confessed to me, "Ethan, I wish I could see myself in our textbook." Inspired by my student's confession, I recognized the urgent need to have a collection of personal stories that empower and offer complex, but truthful, insights into the lives of immigrant, transnational people who are working, living, and contributing their values in the United States.

This edited volume, appropriately titled Critical Storytelling: Multilingual Immigrants in the United States, offers a unique perspective of immigrants living, working, and learning in the United States. These perspectives, in unison, share positive, real, and critical messages of acceptance, acknowledgment, negotiation, and resilience. We believe Critical Storytelling: Multilingual Immigrants in the United States is a wonderful resource for K-12 students as well as for adult learners. Its authentic and powerful message of immigrant resilience is what makes this book interesting and relevant to the diverse population of readers in the United States today.

Book Overview

Critical Storytelling: Multilingual Immigrants in the United States is a beautiful, powerful collection of narratives of multilingual immigrants in the United States. The purpose of this edited book is to create a space where immigrant stories are told from our personal perspectives, using our own voices. We, the contributors of this edited volume, are immigrants from all walks of life who represent a diverse picture of languages, professions, and beliefs from the immigrant diaspora in the United States. Inspired by the use of autoethnography, authors examine our own lives through poems and personal narratives accompanied, in some cases, by drawings or photos. It is our hope that our stories will serve as a bridge between the past, the present, and the future to inspire younger immigrant generations to learn from, honor, and continue recording, or historicizing (see Scott, 1992), their family's truths.

Why Are These Stories Critical?

In 2009, Novelist Chimamanda Ngozi Adichie gave a TEDTalk where she made a case for the danger of a single story. In her talk, she explained that to make a single story about an individual or a culture all that is needed is to "show a people as one thing, as only one thing, over and over again, and that is what they become" (Adichie, 2009). The criticality of the stories shared in *Critical Storytelling: Multilingual Immigrants in the United States* lies in our collective vision to disrupt the single-story narrative about immigrants in the United States. In these chapters, readers will find that we, transnational immigrants, arrive in the United States with diverse, multilingual experiences that make our stories unique. Furthermore, this book is critical because it was purposefully envisioned as an archive to record the transnational, multilingual immigrant stories of our authors and their families. As the editors of this volume, we argue in favor of historicizing immigrant experiences (Scott, 1992). We understand that the work of historicizing the experience of transnational immigrants is a lifelong project and cannot be achieved within the liminal space of this book. For us, this book is just the beginning of a process of recording immigrant experiences and stories with the vision of "honoring people's otherness" (Anzaldúa & Keating, 2002, p. 4) in multiple critical ways.

Suggestions for Using This Book

Our vision is that *Critical Storytelling: Multilingual Immigrants in the United States* can be used in any learning space where adolescent and adult readers are exploring the topic(s) of immigration, inclusion, diversity, languages, culture and cultural diversity, to name a few. In addition, we also believe this edited volume will be a page-turner for readers in the United States from all walks of life as well as those individuals living overseas who are ready to immigrate to the United States and want to learn more about potential cultural negotiations they will experience while living in the United States. In addition, anyone (scholars, teachers, students, researchers, etc.) in the field of language learning, ESOL, bilingual education, social justice, and multicultural education might adopt this text as reading and discussion resources for their classes, including pre- and in-service teacher preparation programs.

How Can You Use Critical Storytelling: Multilingual Immigrants in the United States *in Your Learning Spaces?*

We encourage teachers in middle and high school, as well as educators teaching ESOL to adult learners, to explore the possibility of using this text in their classrooms, whether it be ESOL, English language arts, world language (i.e. Arabic, Spanish, French, Mandarin, etc.), or even in content classes. We believe teachers will find in each chapter of this edited volume a powerful, relatable story their students can use to reflect, discuss, and learn from. Some ideas of how teachers in middle and high school can use this edited book in their learning spaces are:

– *Reading*. Select chapters as in-class reading assignments or homework. When reading, students can practice vocabulary words they already know, learn new ones, and also explore different cultures, customs, and topics that may be new or relatable to their own experiences.
– *Writing*. Ask students to reflect on their reading. You can also ask students to write a response to the author(s) of that chapter or, if they prefer, they can write a reflection on their journals.
– *Speaking*. Give your students the opportunity to discuss in small groups or with the whole class how they felt after reading the chapter(s). You may also create a small-group or whole-class discussion about specific topics addressed in each chapter and ask students to reflect on those topics using their personal experiences and the information shared in the chapter(s).
– *Listening*. As students discuss in class their experiences with the text, ask the other students to actively listen to their peers, and take notes.
– *Summer Reading*. Especially for middle and high school teachers, we recommend this edited book as a book that can be added to your summer reading list. Please share this resource with your school and county leadership and ask them to add it to your summer reading list.

— *Self-Reflection.* Give students time to reflect continuously while they read. In their self-reflections, give them the opportunity to think, record, or write their own stories. For English learners, specifically, personal writing and reflection are empowering practices because they validate their previous experiences (Peregoy & Boyle, 2017). For us, the contributors, the opportunity to use writing to share our stories also became a cathartic, healing process.

Acknowledgments

We would like to express our deepest gratitude and appreciation to every single person who made this book a reality. First, we would like to express our sincere appreciation and gratitude to Dr. Gloria Park for supporting our project and for writing this book's foreword. We would also like to thank Mauricio Patrón Rivera for his support in reviewing the translation of a poem. Furthermore, we are eternally grateful for each of the authors in this beautiful, meaningful collection. All of us are individuals dealing with daily struggles and challenges, yet, we carved time to share our stories in this space. Lastly, we would like to extend our gratitude to the series editors, Nicholas Hartlep and Brandon Hensley, for their trust in this project.

References

Adichie, N. C. (2009, July). The danger of a single story [Video file]. https://www.ted.com/talks/chimamanda_ngozi_adichie_the_danger_of_a_single_story?utm_content=talk&utm_source=linkedin.com&utm_medium=referral&utm_term=social-science&utm_campaign=social

Anzaldúa, G., & Keating, A. (2002). *This bridge we call home: Radical visions for transformation.* Routledge.

Peregoy, S. F., & Boyle, O. F. (2017). *Reading, writing, and learning in ESL: A resource book for K-12 teachers* (7th ed.). Longman.

Scott, J. W. (1992). Experience. In J. Butler & J. W. Scott (Eds.), *Feminists theorize the political* (pp. 22–40). Routledge.

Figures

Notes on Contributors

Editors

Luis Javier Pentón Herrera
(PhD) is a Dissertation Core Faculty in the Department of Educational Leadership and Administration at the American College of Education and an adjunct professor at The George Washington University and University of Maryland Global Campus. In addition, he serves as the Social Responsibility Interest Section (SRIS) Co-Chair elect and as a member of the Affiliate Network Professional Council at TESOL International Association. Dr. Pentón Herrera's current research projects focus on the language and literacy experiences of adolescent and adult Indigenous Latinx students in U.S. classrooms and on adolescent and adult Latinx students with limited or interrupted formal education (SLIFE). In addition, he is also exploring the topics of moral values, healing, emotions, and humane learning in K-12 language learning spaces. Originally from La Habana, Cuba, Luis enjoys running, writing, and spending all his free time with his two doggies Maui and Virgo.

Ethan Tính Trịnh
(they/them) is a Vietnamese queer immigrant who is passionate about teaching marginalized queer and trans youths of color and learning about queer teachers' identities. They are an activist, an educator, a Chicana-feminist writer, and a decolonial researcher. Their major influences include Gloria Anzaldúa and Thích Nhất Hạnh. They are pursuing a PhD in Middle and Secondary Education at Georgia State University, with a minor in Women's and Gender Studies. Ethan's work focuses on the intersectionality of gender, race, and language education that embraces queerness as a healing teaching and research practice. Ethan has published in a wide range of international journals, including *International Journal of Qualitative Studies in Education*, *LGBTQ Policy Journal*, *Camino Real. Estudios de las Hispanidades Norteamericanas*, *Genealogy* as well as other book chapters. Originally from Mekong Delta, Vietnam, Ethan enjoys creative writing while having a cup of Vietnamese iced coffee with milk or cà phê sữa đá to kick off their mornings.

Authors

Gabriel T. Acevedo Velázquez
is an Assistant Professor in English Education in the English Department at Arizona State University. His identities as a Latinx, Bilingual, and Queer educator

in Puerto Rico and the United States inform his research and creative writing. He was born and raised in Puerto Rico and also taught English Language Arts, English as a Second Language and Theater in elementary and secondary levels while also addressing significant social issues with his students. His research interests focus on Teacher Education, Bilingualism, Spanglish, (Queer) Young Adult Literature, Pop-Culture Pedagogies, and Creative Writing.

Fatmeh Alalawneh

is a third-year doctoral student in the Curriculum and Instruction Program at the University of Toledo. Her research interests include adult ESL education, issues of access, diversity, and equity in higher education. She has over ten years of experience teaching EFL/ESL courses in Jordan and the United States. For the past four years, she has been involved with helping refugees and immigrants learn English and develop their professional careers.

Bashar Al Hariri

is a Visiting Assistant Professor of English at the University of Toledo, where he teaches ESL composition and linguistics classes. He also coordinates the ESL program at US Together Refugee Resettlement Agency, where he teaches multilevel ESL courses to newly resettled refugees and immigrants in Toledo. His research interests include refugee and adult education, ESL writing, and identity in second language learning.

Rajwan Alshareefy

is PhD student in the Composition and Applied Linguistics program at Indiana University of Pennsylvania (IUP). He taught English in high school and in college in Iraq. He also worked as a Teaching Associate of composition at IUP between 2018–2020. His research interests include transnationalism, identity, composition, second language teaching, and critical discourse analysis.

Ana Bautista

is 41 years old and was born on March 22nd, 1979. Ana comes from a beautiful city called Moniquirá, Boyacá (Colombia), and currently lives in the city of Atlanta, USA. She is a volunteer teacher at the Centro Hispano Marista, an educational institution that promotes General Educational Development (GED), supporting the area of Language. Ana graduated from Universidad Externado de Colombia with the title of Master in Education and has a working career in the field of education of more than 15 years in Colombia, but for reasons adverse to her will, she had to emigrate to the United States. Ana shares an autobiographical poem for this valuable project.

May F. Chung

is the Assistant Professor in Academic Writing for the International Fellows at the National Defense University. As a writing teacher, Ms. May specializes in second language pedagogy and incorporating students' native languages into composition. She received her Bachelors in English Education and English as a Second Language at North Carolina State University, where she also received her Master's in English Sociolinguistics. She is currently finishing her doctorate degree in Language, Literacy, and Culture at the University of Maryland, Baltimore County.

Zurisaray Espinosa

is a doctoral student at GSU with a concentration in Language and Literacy in the department of Middle and Secondary education. She is a former certified high school Spanish and English teacher with a B.A. in English Literature and an M.A.T. in Teaching English: Secondary Education (Grades 6–12). Her future research will focus on mindfulness-based practices that are influenced by Chicana Feminism and Indigenous knowledges and how those practices may be implemented in urban ESOL classroom contexts.

Manuel De Jesús Gómez Portillo

is an educator, researcher, a life-long learner, and a supporter of equal rights for all. Manuel was born in El Salvador, moved to the United States at the age of 10 and settled in Virginia. He received a degree in Psychology from Radford University and a Master's degree in TESOL from Shenandoah University. Manuel has taught in China and in Virginia. He is working on his doctorate degree in educational leadership from Shenandoah University and his research interests include family engagement, cultural wealth of minorities, and college and career readiness for minority students and parents.

Jamie Harris

is an adult education professional for over 13 years and has worked in English for Speakers of Other Languages, English as a Foreign Language, Adult Basic Education, and teacher trainer programs, nationally and internationally. Working with adult learners has been an extension of Jamie's desire to support the success of adult learners with significant barriers. Jamie currently serves as the First Vice President of Maryland TESOL and works as an Education Program Specialist for the state of Maryland with a specialty in technology integration. Mrs. Harris has a B.S. in Communication Studies and a M.Ed. in Adult Education, TESOL.

Ben Haseen

is a Bengali American immigrant and a transgender activist residing in Atlanta, GA. He is a medical student attending Morehouse School of Medicine and is slated to become the first openly transgender physician of South Asian descent in the United States. He has published works in literary analysis, public health research, and queer activism. He hopes to one day practice medicine helping underserved populations and advocating for universal healthcare rights. Currently Ben is the communications co-chair in the Atlanta based organization, Atlanta Queer and Asian Community.

Lydiah Kananu Kiramba

(PhD) is an assistant professor of educational linguistics in the Department of Teaching, Learning and Teacher education at the University of Nebraska-Lincoln. Her research examines communicative practices of multilingual/multicultural students in super-diverse classrooms, and literacies of migrants, immigrants and multilingual populations in K-12 classrooms.

Babak Khoshnevisan

is a PhD in the Technology in Education and Second Language Acquisition (TESLA) Program at the University of South Florida (USF). He is a teacher educator of ESOL courses at USF. He also teaches EAP courses to international students at INTO USF. His research interests include but not are not limited to teacher education, idiomaticity, developmental stages of teachers, and CALL.

Sharada Krishnamurthy

is a doctoral candidate in Language, Literacy and Socio-cultural Education at Rowan University. She is working on her dissertation on translingual literacies and anti-racist practices in writing centers. Her research interests include challenging monolingual ideologies and creating equitable and inclusive spaces for language minoritized students in higher education. She has taught education classes in linguistics and second language acquisition, teaching linguistically diverse students, and human exceptionality. As a former writing center director, she has experience tutoring writing and teaching first year writing and composition. She is also an avid reader and writer of short stories and poetry.

Judith Landeros

(she/her) is a rising third year PhD student in the Cultural Studies in Education program in Curriculum and Instruction at UT Austin. She studies the inclusion of Critical Indigenous Studies, Ethnic Studies and Land as pedagogy within teacher preparation education programs. She is also interested in the identity formation of bi/multilingual P-12 students, particularly children and youth who identify as Latinx and/or Indigenous.

Jiyoon Lee

(PhD) is an assistant professor of TESOL in the Department of Education at the University of Maryland, Baltimore County (UMBC). She works closely with pre- and in-service teachers in her research and teaching. She was born and raised in South Korea and completed her master's in TESOL and PhD in Educational Linguistics in the U.S.A. She has been always interested in learning languages. Other than English and Korean, she has learned German and Mandarin at high school and Spanish and Cantonese in her adult life.

Pablo Montes

is a PhD student at the University of Texas at Austin. He is the son of migrant workers from Guanajuato, Mexico, and currently works with the Coahuiltecan community in central Texas. His research interests include the intersection of queer settler colonialism, Indigeneity, and Land education.

Aracelis Nieves

(PhD) is a Spanish language educator, researcher, and published author. She is passionate about the conception of an equitable and just education for all students. Particularly, her research contributes to the fields of critical language pedagogy, culturally responsive pedagogy, student-centered curriculum, and exemplary programs for heritage language learners. Dr. Nieves has presented widely about those topics at international conferences in the United States, Puerto Rico, and Spain. Her ideas have been well received by the American Council for the Teaching of Foreign Languages, and the National Association of Bilingual Education. Correspondingly, they have published articles about her research in their journals.

Gloria Park

is a professor and graduate director of the Graduate Studies in Composition and Applied Linguistics housed in the English Department at Indiana University of Pennsylvania in PA, USA. Her work centers around critical perspectives on language teacher identity, teacher education, and social justice-oriented teacher inquiry. She has recently begun a large scale ethnographic inquiry focusing on transnational family stories. As such, her major work has appeared in journals such as *TESOL Quarterly*, *TESOL Journal, Journal of Language, Identity and Education, Race, Ethnicity and Education*, *ELT Journal* as well as in numerous edited volumes. Her most recent monograph, Narratives of East Asian

Women Teachers of English: Where Privilege Meets Marginalization, was published by Multilingual Matters in 2017.

Mauricio Patrón Rivera
(Mexico City, 1984) writes about outsider corporalities. He usually do collaborative work. He is doing a PhD in Creative Writing in Spanish at the University of Houston. He likes to do curatorial research, translation, social communication, and journalism. Right now, he is overcoming a cynical stage.

Tairan Qiu
is a doctoral student in the Department of Language and Literacy Education at the University of Georgia. Her research interests are oriented around exploring the multiliteracy practices of transnational youths, centering their stories, and advocating for more opportunities in their schools, communities, and homes to sustain their entire cultural, linguistic, and literacy repertoires. Her scholarship has appeared in *Written Communication, Journal of Language and Literacy Education,* and *The Qualitative Report.* Tairan was born and mostly raised in Kunming, Yunnan, China. In her free time, she loves cooking, hiking, swimming, and spending time with her husband and dog.

R. Joseph Rodríguez
is of U.S.-Mexican descent and was born and raised in Houston, Texas. He attended public schools and is a graduate of Kenyon College. His most recent book projects are *This Is Our Summons Now: Poems* and *Adolescent Scribes: Teaching a Love of Writing.* Joseph is coeditor of *English Journal.* He lives in Austin, Texas. Follow him @escribescribe

Cristina Sánchez-Martín
is assistant professor in the Composition and Applied Linguistics and MA TESOL programs at Indiana University of Pennsylvania, where she does research on and teaches about writing, language, and identity from a transnational perspective.

Sandy "San" Tadeo
(he/him/his) immigrated to the United States, as he was obliged to pack and follow his parents when they moved from the Philippines to Hawai'i at the turn of the century. He attended a public high school that was located on top of a mountain, overlooking the Pacific Ocean, then joined the U.S. Marine Corps unbeknown to his parents. After graduating with a master's degree in IT, he is now a digital media analyst at one of the US federal agencies' communications

office, serving Veterans, service members, and their families. His ambition is to continue with his studies and obtain an MBA in the near future.

Geovanny Vicente Romero

is a columnist for CNN based in Washington, DC. He is a political strategist, international consultant and lecturer. He has published many articles on development, human rights, governance, democracy, elections, the environment, as well as the role of women in a society. He is the founder of the Dominican Republic Center of Public Policy, Leadership and Development (CPDL-RD). Geovanny has a master's degree from The George Washington University in political communications and strategic governance. His Twitter is @GeovannyVicentR

Polina Vinogradova

(PhD) is Director of the TESOL Program at American University in Washington, DC. Her research focuses on the use of digital stories in language education and on postmethod pedagogy and advocacy in language teacher development. She is a co-editor (with Joan Kang Shin) of *Contemporary Foundations for Teaching English as an Additional Language: Pedagogical Approaches and Classroom Applications* (Routledge, 2021). She holds a PhD in Language, Literacy, and Culture and MA in Intercultural Communication from the University of Maryland, Baltimore County, and MA in TESOL from the University of Northern Iowa.

PART 1

POETRY

∴

Immigrant Background Students' Names and Identities in U.S. Schools: Voices from the Underground

This poem is a recreation of conversational interviews with five immigrant background adolescent African girls (Pendo, Furaha, Amani, Faraja, and Neema), all names are pseudonyms. In those interviews, the girls continuously shared how important their names are for them and the challenges they encountered with teachers and peers mispronouncing their names. One student mentioned taking time to teach her teachers, but was often told, "It's just a name." Weird gazes on her teachers' faces are the best pronunciation she had received.

This free verse poem speaks to the relationship between students' individual names and identities, biases—which are often based on language hierarchies and power—in learning names, the peer pressure some parents and teens have to get anglicized names in order to belong, and the position some students find themselves in, whether resisting or conforming, whether with support from others or not. This piece, therefore, is a request to all educators to realize that students' names are not just labels or registration numbers. They carry a deeper meaning—of identity, lineage, history—which we are all tasked to honor and appreciate.

It's Just a Name! Voices from the Underground

My name, my precious name
It defines me for who I am
My ethnicity and my character
All giving me a place in this world
From the time I was born to the time I die,
My name will be who I am.

© KONINKLIJKE BRILL NV, LEIDEN, 2021 | DOI: 10.1163/9789004446182_001

First mispronunciation of my name,
I assured myself
It is the first time a name like mine existed in print.
I decide I will teach them my name
I teach each one at a time.
Beginning with my teacher
Once, twice, thrice! Lol!
It is too difficult for me, I hear
Shrugs shoulders!
All year-round, it is difficult
Get used to it, I hear
It's just a name!

Why can't you take the time to learn my name?
With sadness, I ask myself.
Maybe it is a difficult name? Maybe?
No! It is a name in an illegitimate language!
A language of peasants
Deserving neither honor nor mention
In a world of linguistic hierarchies.

What if it was a French name?
What if it was a German name?
Portuguese even?
Perhaps then, only perhaps,
It would be interesting to learn
To sound it out right.
It is a cool thing,
to at least get a single word right
in these powerful languages.
But not in my invisible tongue
The peasants' tongue.

Patience escapes me daily.
I cannot tolerate it anymore.
I feel unrecognized like I do not exist.
My name is too difficult and complex to learn,
Even the school geniuses cannot learn my name.
Is it by choice or volition?
Do they need to?

One semester goes
Over 100 times I remember teaching my name
No one gets it right, oh wait!
No, just a few do. Those who care to
Those who see me
Not as a registration label
But human, deserving my ancestral dignity

The second semester begins
Voices from the underground are amplified
Get an American name
Only then will you belong
I think to myself, that is right.
Madison, Maude, Natalie,
all these are easy, beautiful names, are they not?!

The battle of the Titans in my little mind.
Each day is a sad day for me
A weird gaze from my teacher's face
Defines my name, I sound it out, like a soliloquy
For fear and embarrassment engulf me
It is a few peers' chances to make fun of me

Maybe, I need an anglicized name, I say to myself
To belong, to fit in, to be appreciated, to be seen
My parents say it may cause my ancestors to turn in their graves
I do not want that!
I persuade myself, *it is just a name.*
I stop trying to teach it, to the unteachable
With sadness, I say, *it is just a name!*

It is just a name!
The cry of the unseen
Invisible and marginalized
Seen from a *colonial gaze*
Like a cliché, I lose meaning

Who am I? I ask.
Can I just be?
I resolve I am me.

Daughter of a peasant farmer
Melanistic African queen
Bearing my Indigenous names and roots.

I resolve I am me
Defying erasure of my own identity
Defying erasure of my history
Before my own eyes
Celebrating the beauty of my name
My language, my culture, my tales, my beauty.

My name is my history
It is not just a registration label,
It has a cultural meaning
In my beautiful language
Rich with phonetic sounds
Do not make me conform to the former colonial masters' phonetics
I do not want to be lost in the mirage of things
I do not want to annoy my ancestors.

My name is a rebirth of my great grandparents
Stop silencing their voices through me
Do you not see?
I am a walking history
Of tales told and untold
Of worlds wildest dreams
Those of my ancestors

Author Commentary

Names are an important part of each person's identity. Names carry important and intricate webs and networks of meaning, such that anglicizing or shortening those names without consent amounts to attempts to erase a part of individuals' identity. When children are moving away from everything they know and immigrate to the United States, oftentimes one of the only things from their culture that they have left to hold onto is their name.

Research has continuously documented the importance of positive identity to school success and the relationship between student names and identity (Dion, 1983; Kiramba & Oloo, 2019). A study by Dion (1983) on the psychology behind the relationship of names and identity demonstrated that when young adults and children were asked, the question, "who am I?", young adults responded with categories of name, sex, or familial roles; while the "younger children mentioned their names first" (1983, p. 248); in other words, children describe who they are with their names. Dion concluded that many children predicated their feeling of continuity from "the past to the present and into the future on the fact of retaining the same name" (1983, p. 249). Guardo and Bohan (1971) found that children viewed their names as an anchor to their personal identities. Thus, a negative view of one's own identity could impact both academic and social success for students. Names frequently carry cultural or family significance and can connect children to their cultures or ancestors, as the girls in this poem suggested. Thus, mispronouncing students' names frequently throughout childhood can negate the history and significance of their names, and thus the identity of the child (Kohli & Solórzano, 2012).

The impact of mispronouncing names on students of color is huge. Considering that there is a strong connection between name and identity when their names are mispronounced, hence misrepresented, one's identity can begin to feel shaky as a result. When students hear their names continuously mispronounced by their teachers and peers, they feel as if their culture is being looked down upon, as less than (Kohli & Solórzano, 2012). The students of the poem shared in this chapter that they felt invisible. More so, the girls' voices in the poem reference names in languages that are considered powerful, such as French, German, Portuguese, where names are respected and learned as compared to names in African languages. The girls in this poem perceived the socioeconomic capital and hierarchical nature of languages (Kiramba, 2018), thus, mispronouncing their names meant they did not belong.

When students feel like their culture is not valued by their teachers and peers, they begin to question the worth of their cultural values. While some of the girls changed their names in order to fit in, to belong to the American culture, and to avoid having to teach it every day to their teachers and peers, others learned to hate their names. Keller and Franzak (2016) discussing the implications of students not finding their own names in literature or picture books, shared an example of a book talk about a boy named Bilal, who insisted on being called Bill because he "recognizes that his name signifies an identity unwelcomed at school" (p. 4). Immigrant students, like any other student, want to fit in with their peers, but this pressure to fit in is different for them than it is for their peers. For younger students, having a name that their teacher cannot pronounce, brings grief and embarrassment, as one of the girls noted.

Kohli and Solórzano (2012) share multiple stories about students that asked to go by different names to avoid their teachers' struggle to pronounce their names. Mispronouncing names may lead to some students developing anxiety and a deep-rooted resentment for their names. Many students do not have the confidence or tools to stand up to an unfamiliar environment of teachers and peers who are different from them, hence their voices remain underground. And, while students in minoritized groups will hope that anglicizing their names can lessen discrimination, research instead shows that students with a higher sense of identity have higher chances of doing well academically. This poem is a call for all educators—let's all strive to learn one another's names.

References

Dion, K. L. (1983). Names, identity and self. *Names: A Journal of Onomastics, 31*(4), 245–257. doi:10.1179/nam.1983.31.4.245

Guardo, C. J., & Bohan, J. B. (1971). Development of a sense of self-identity in children. *Child Development, 42*, 1909–1921.

Keller, T., & Franzak, J. K. (2016). When names and schools collide: Critically analyzing depictions of culturally and linguistically diverse children negotiating their names in picture books. *Children's Literature in Education, 47*(2), 177–190.

Kiramba, L. K. (2018). Language ideologies and epistemic exclusion, *Language and Education, 32*(4), 291–312. doi:10.1080/09500782.2018.1438469

Kiramba, L. K., & Oloo, J. A. (2019). "It's OK. She doesn't even speak English." Narratives of language, culture, and identity negotiation by immigrant high school students. *Urban Education.* https://doi.org/10.1177/0042085919873696

Kohli, R., & Solórzano, D. G. (2012). Teachers, please learn our names! Racial micro-aggressions and the K-12 classroom. *Race Ethnicity and Education, 15*(4), 441–462. doi:10.10080/13613324.2012.674026

CHAPTER 2

This Is Our Summons Now

R. Joseph Rodríguez

Poetry can invite readers to experience language in many forms and also to gain insights into the experiences of fellow humans. Through a poem, a reader's experiences and emotions can come alive and provide new meanings.

The poems selected here are from a manuscript I titled *This Is Our Summons Now*. The title is meant to be a calling or order for readers to act for change and hope as witnesses of the times in which we live. Readers must attend to their duty for a change. Each poem was written in a state of urgency and also as a plea to pay attention and act in ways that lead to hope and justice.

Everyjuan/x

arises
before coffee drips
everywhere
faces grace hell
idle justice
knows limits
memorizes
notices
opportunities
permanent
qualification
restores
sanity
thinks
underdog
vows
winning
xenagogue
yearns
zapateo

"Everyjuan/x" praises the manual labor and unnoticed contributions of many diverse U.S. migrants who continue the journey through resilience and solidarity, despite the current state of deportation, dehumanization, and fear they face. Hope appears as many advocates and citizens become upstanders against the hate and xenophobia in our communities and media.

A Teacher Dreams with His Students

In the beginning, there is light
and two wide-eyed figures standing
near the foot of your bed,
and the sound of their voices is love.
(Matt de la Peña, from *Love*, 2018)

Tue., 5th September 2017

Dear Students and Teachers,
I open my journal to write about my teaching day.
My students tell me their summons will come.
Their crime is to fulfill their dream of learning
in this country, they and others now call home.

And what do I tell them tomorrow when I write
on the whiteboard an essential question for the day?
Who's essential? Who survives? Who cares?
And who declares which Dreamers can stay?

Cautiously you tell me your mornings begin.
Each early dawn brings many fears and plans.
Each day comes with a horizon and sundown.
Hope you carry high in your hearts and hands.

Another semester will come, and this classroom
is our safe and keeping place. Come, stay here.
Your dreams and journeys are yours and ours.
As your teacher, I will be the hull and steer.

"A teacher dreams with his students" speaks to the change and hope that teachers bring daily to children and adolescents in our schools. In particular, this poem

*highlights how our students' lives and dreams are worthy in our classrooms and
how they seek dignified treatment as lawful citizens.*

Homeland Insecurity

US builds migrant tent city in Texas as Trump likens influx to 'Disneyland'.
(headline from *The Guardian*, 29 April 2019)

Dear Policymakers, Políticos, and Congress in Regress:

Free the children, mothers, and fathers

from your grip and contracts.

The USA still occupies and extorts their lands.

Bring our children, mothers, and fathers home.
This is our summons now.

We await your promise
of freedom in compromised lands.

Sincerely,
We the People
(across the USA and abroad)

Galut

at Tornillo

A chorus of citizens
quilt the children
under tents
in the cold.

The children wait
in cages
for mothers

and fathers moving
across continental plates.

Here arms outstretch,
far from Galilee
in the Chihuahuan Desert
winter and creosote.

The chorus rises—flor
y canto—for the children
coming home
at last
to be clothed
in familiar warmth
and love.

"Homeland Insecurity" and "Galut" attempt to change the narrative by providing lenses into the national and international policies that criminalize, dehumanize, and incarcerate children, adolescents, and families. Refugees seek shelter daily in the United States and around the world. As neighbors and citizens of the world, we can offer them freedom and rays of hope for survival.

Anthem

Oh, America, can you see and notice us, standing before you?
On your lands and shores, we arrive: tossed into detention
for a place at your table and in your pages of history.
Who's a pioneer or settler now? We migrate to your door
for inalienable rights and truths so self-evident.
Stories you cover and hide like our face and labor.
See us now and be the liberty that enlightens the world.

"Anthem" challenges the U.S. national anthem in favor of a hopeful narrative that seeks action. America can stand for equal opportunity, freedom, hope, and justice as depicted in the Statue of Liberty, a gift from the French in 1886 and a national monument, which was originally named Liberty Enlightening the World.

If Walt Whitman

happened to round
the corner
or just sit
on my front porch
to celebrate the songs
of himself
and the multitudes
among us
would it be
a good idea
to call the cops
to round him up
and carry him off
for panhandling
and soliciting
his poems
as he does so boldly
hugging the world
we call *home*?

yes, he carries
some bags
with papers
pencils
holes
oranges
nuts
like a bread giver.

well, who knows
what i'd do
if he tries
to move on in
and set-up shop
with a loan
from the small

business people's
administration
and open a poetry pantry.

oooooh, right now
the next-door neighbor's got
one of those handheld cameras
on us
with live feed
as she dials 9-1-1
all techy crazed.

oh, boy, really?!
she's made it
her doggone business
to broadcast us.
so i best just sit
and chill here
beside walt
as we get
fully broadcasted,
sin permiso,
mind you,
to the whole wide world
that's always awake
and stirring the pot
all hidden with aliases
behind glowing screens.

just to be clear, officer,
drop that weapon
you're holding:
fellow travelers, are we
who are bound
on our merry way
like troubadours
with flower and song
on a pilgrimage
across many towns?

"If walt whitman" invites readers to experience change and hope through a counternarrative about U.S. poetry and society. In fact, the migrant-poet-pilgrim-traveler-troubadour, Walt Whitman, and others seek shelter, understanding, and allies to make a better world for themselves and those who shall follow.

CHAPTER 3

Gringo or Rican or Just Me

Gabriel Teodoro Acevedo Velázquez

Being a light-skinned Puerto Rican affords me great privileges. As a United States citizen, opportunities for freedom of expression and freedom of speech come with the territory. However, U.S. citizenship also comes with confusion when it comes to individual identities. This poem highlights the personal choices of whitewashing my name in order to make it easier for others to address me. Also, this piece shows off my personal struggles with reaffirming my Puerto Rican identity.

> In school, I learned a lot more about other people's last names
> rather than the ones closer to my own.
> As if González, Acevedo or Velázquez
> were much harder to pronounce than Kerouac, Einstein, or Rowling.
> It is like our last names were made of straitjackets, constraining the hands
> of those trying to conquer the dream they were promised.
>
> See, my mother named me Gabriel Teodoro but, honestly,
> I always hated the name, Gabriel Teodoro.
> Being a young Puerto Rican boy,
> being told to speak English,
> and being encouraged to be white,
> it was hard for me to make the connection through my name.
> I realized my name did not match my background, even before I knew how to spell
> c-o-l-o-n-i-z-a-t-i-o-n.
>
> I always wanted a name that set the bar high,
> that tumbled out of the mouth,
> that somersaulted into a room,
> that split the air,
> that afforded me privileges,
> a name like James or George.
> Although I must have punched inside the placenta,
> my parents decided on something mixed.

© KONINKLIJKE BRILL NV, LEIDEN, 2021 | DOI: 10.1163/9789004446182_003

A first name associated with an angel,
and a middle name meaning "gift from God."
A name full of grace,
a name easily washed down with café con leche
and, although I speak English, I am from Puerto Rico.
¡Boricua! ¡Puñeta! ¡Ay, bendito! ¡Algarete! ¡Jíbaro!

Your name is a song
so now I call myself Gabo.
I wanted a name that reminded me of the beautiful hills in Puerto Rico
rising
and campesinos uprising
and estudiantes protestando
and millions screaming "¡RICKY RENUNCIA!"
Con ollas y cacerolas en mano.

The funny thing is I changed my pronunciation to Gabe
so colonizers have less to hold on to.
In Puerto Rico all your names are important,
because there is an emphasis on family.
But in the USA, your nickname comes first
because there is an emphasis on accessibility.
I had to dumb down my identity so I could fit into a closed-box society.
On countless occasions, I have introduced myself
and people would say things like:
"But what's your real name?"
and "You don't look Latino."
Easy, that is because my nickname was not given to me.
It was given to all of you
so that when you hear Gabe you hear class, power, and whiteness;
but names like Manolito, Neftalí, and Santiago
sound foreign, impoverished, illegal, not white.

Your name is scary,
it is a black hole.
But what they do not know is that
black holes are the brightest source of light.
I used to wish my name was generic,
Something like Spencer Miller.
A heavy name with thick syllables

shut down with short blades
so, when I have my own kids,
I could name them something special.

Something to make people stumble on!
Something to make their skin thicker than mine!
Something to remind the people around them about El Grito de Lares y
El Cerro Maravilla!
Something Powerful!
Something Ethnic!
Something Unforgettable!
Something Boricua!

Being Boricua is difficult. Whether you were born and raised in Puerto Rico, born in the island but raised in the States, or born and raised in the U.S. but with Puerto Rican identities, the struggle of finding who you are is always present. For Latinx communities in the States, the mythical images of light-skinned, blonde-haired, blue-eyed people are constantly being thrown in our faces. I find myself engaging in inner conversations on how to negotiate who I am with what society wants me to be.

This poem seeks to enlighten a sense of nostalgia and Puerto Rican patri-otism in readers by acknowledging changes we engage in by presenting our-selves differently. For any Latinx, especially Puerto Rican youth who come across this poem, I assure you that who *you* are matters, that *your* voice and *your* name matter. You will be put to the test many times and in those trying situations you might choose to change aspects of yourselves to fit whatever current narrative serves you best. However, rest assured that there is nothing more beautiful and amazing than who you are and maybe it is today or ten years from now when you realize that but whenever you do, it will be the right time for you.

Sincerely,
GABO

CHAPTER 4

Spaces in Between

Sharada Krishnamurthy

When I came to the United States as an international student from India many years ago, I was struck with wonder about the wide-open spaces, pristine and neat, and with the people who seemed friendly and welcoming. It was such a contrast to the chaotic, messy, and colorful country I came from. Growing up in India, our family moved every few years to a new town in a different state. Each new place meant a period of adjustment, getting used to a new language and new cuisine, making new friends, and always feeling like an outsider.

When I finally came to the United States, it was by choice, and I thought this land of equal opportunity for all was the perfect place for me to make my home. But soon I realized that this country was not a benevolent meritocracy where one could shine regardless of race, color, or language. The discrimination and distancing were subtle but very present. Slowly, I became disillusioned by this country's insular thinking and superior attitude toward other nations and peoples. I struggled to fit in and feel at home. I had to let go of this myth of the great United States as a melting pot where everyone belonged. But, over time, I learned to love the wonderful things about this country—the freedoms, the clean air, the abundance of open spaces—and challenge the discrimination and inequities. Most importantly I learned to embrace who I am! This poem titled *Spaces in Between* reflects my journey of self-discovery, and of moving through different places to carve my own space.

Spaces in Between

I have always existed in spaces in between
not quite a Tamilian, nor a Maharashtrian, nor a Gujarati
my language a mishmash of tongues
words sprinkled from here and there that marked me as different
I was a "rendungattan," as my mother would say.
Going to Madras, mocked by my relatives for my lack of Tamil skills
But that was okay because I spoke English better
Stiff Upper Lip and all!

© KONINKLIJKE BRILL NV, LEIDEN, 2021 | DOI: 10.1163/9789004446182_004

Privileging the colonizer's tongue over my native ones
because English symbolized education and erudition and culture.

Culture! How ironic that I thought traditions of clotted cream and
crumpets were something to aspire for! How could my tongue, soaked
in the spicy chutneys and "urugai" and "chaats" ever be content with the
blandness of cuisines in faraway lands!
And in Bombay, I was always a Madrasi,
"unda gunda po"—the nonsensical gibberish that non-South Indians
spew to mock and mark the darkies!
the country south of the Vindhyas
marked by my skin, too dark to elicit approval
both inside and outside the home
"Karuppu!"
"Kaali!"
and I continued to exist between here and there and nowhere.

Arriving in the United States
in the promised land or so I thought
where your skin, your tongue, your culture did not matter
as much as your knowledge and hard work
But *no , no, no!*
the disdain, the disrespect, the discrimination
all there too subtle for me to see at first
Questions, seemingly innocent, "Did you go to school on an elephant?"
"I know you live in New Jersey but where are you really from?"
Comments, supposedly complimentary, "You don't have an Indian
accent!"
"You speak English/French so well!"
I did not understand why these questions, these comments made me
uncomfortable
I did not have words to describe them
Microaggressions
I learned that term later
These ways of making it known that I was different, not one of them
my face flushed dark (can my face get darker??)
with shame and disappointment
I DON'T BELONG!

Existing in limbo
Without a homeland
Wondering where I belong
Slowly unlearning the Eurocentric narratives
Freeing my colonized mind
Embracing who I am, where I am.

I am a mongrel
I am a hybrid
I am from here, there and everywhere
Moving between spaces
Creating space
Making it my own
Tanglish, Hinglish, Frenchish
thaiyir saadam, urugai, bhel puri,
strawberries and whipped cream
pizza and pecan pie
My tongue, *no, my tongues*
Twisting, unfolding
Serpentine and sage
Doing a happy dance
Living in the *spaces in between*

I wrote this poem in response to a "Where I am from" prompt in my graduate class on multilingual literacies. I learned so much in this class about the challenges that racially, linguistically, and culturally diverse people in the United States face. Additionally, being in a doctoral program focused on equity, access, and success, taught me how to become an advocate for language and cultural diversity, and strive for equity for all people. I see this poem as a celebration of diversity and difference for all those individuals who, like me, find themselves living in the spaces in between.

CHAPTER 5

"¡Vamos Mijo, I Know You Can Do This!"

Manuel De Jesús Gómez Portillo

The first day of college for a first-generation immigrant in the United States can be an overwhelming experience. As the first person in the family to go to college, there is a great deal of pressure from family members, friends, and members of the community to succeed. However, a mother's *consejos*[1] can often provide comfort and advice during this unique experience. This poem highlights how my mother's *consejos* and aspirational capital[2] provided me with guidance, courage, and comfort on the day that I left for college in the United States.

> *¡Despiértate, ya es tiempo!*
> Were the first words that my mother uttered with excitement in the
> morning that I was moving away for college.
> I was nervous
> I was scared
> I was petrified
> I only slept an hour or two during the previous night.
>
> *¿Estás nervioso?*
> As we packed all of my belongings into the car, my mom noticed that I
> was shaking.
> I was anxious
> I was frightened
> I was sad
> As the first person in my family to do this, I did not know what to expect.
>
> *Ven mijo, toma un cafecito con pan.*
> As my mother noticed how nervous I was, she comforted me with food
> and coffee.
> I smiled nervously
> I thanked her
> I looked down
> I started to cry
> My emotions were all over the place and I began to question my ability
> to succeed in college.

© KONINKLIJKE BRILL NV, LEIDEN, 2021 | DOI: 10.1163/9789004446182_005

¡Estoy orgullosa de ti!
As I sat down to drink coffee with *pan salvadoreño*,[3] my mother expressed how proud she was of me.
I was warm
I was cheered
I was hopeful
My mother's encouraging words gave me the courage to keep going.

¡Vámonos, es hora de irnos!
As we got in the car to embark on the four-hour journey, my nerves got worse.
I was shaking
I was sad
I was crying
As we left our house, I said goodbye for the second time to a familiar and comforting place.

No estés triste mijo
As we said goodbye to familiar sights and drove into a foreign land, my mother tried to comfort me again.
I was alone
I was cold
I was an alien
Emotions similar to how I felt when I left my *pulgarcito*,
[4] El Salvador, had returned.

En nuestra familia, tú eres el futuro
As we were about to arrive, my mother's words provided me with comfort and pressure at the same time.
I was encouraged
I was anxious
I was nervous
Although her words encouraged me, I felt pressured, as I was the first person in my entire family to go to college. They were all depending on my success.

¡Ya llegamos, que bonita la universidad!
After a long drive, we finally arrived at the place that would be my home for the next four years.

I was tense
I was optimistic
I was scared
The beautiful campus made me feel nervous, yet hopeful. I did not know what to expect in my new and foreign home.

¡Vamos mijo, yo sé que puedes hacerlo!
As we unpacked all of my belongings into my college dorm, my mother's *consejos* provided me with hope.
I was inspired
I was comforted
I was encouraged

Although I was nervous, hearing my mother's *consejos* gave me the courage needed to start a new and exciting journey in the United States. Despite the fact that I was unsure as to what the next four years would bring, I knew that I felt proud to be the first person in my family to go to college.

Final Thoughts

Being the first person to go to college in their families can be an exciting and nerve-wracking experience for immigrants in the United States. For many Latinx first-generation college students, their parents' aspirational capital (Yosso, 2005) can provide words of security and support. The aspirational words of hope and determination mentioned by Latinx parents not only provide Latinx college-bound students with encouragement, but also with inspiration. Often, the aspirations that many Latinx students have are also the dreams of their parents.

The purpose of this poem is to give readers insight on the experiences that immigrant students feel on their first day of college in the United States. For those who read this poem, my hope is you will feel how my mother's encouraging *consejos* offered me with a sense of reassurance. My mother's *consejos* not only gave me comfort and guidance, but also love, which in return provided me with a great deal of courage and strength during such an imperative event in my life. This poem is dedicated to my mother, María Mabel Gómez Portillo and to all of the immigrant parents who never give up and always provide their children with unconditional love and support.

Notes

1　In Spanish, the word *consejos* means advice.
2　According to Yosso (2005), aspirational capital is defined as "the ability to maintain hopes and dreams for the future, even in the face of real and perceived barriers" (p. 77).
3　A type of bread from El Salvador that is usually eaten for breakfast.
4　El Salvador is commonly known as el pulgarcito or "the thumb" of America. This term of endearment is used because El Salvador is the smallest country in Central America.

Reference

Yosso, T. (2005). Whose culture has capital? A critical race theory discussion on community cultural wealth. *Race Ethnicity and Education, 8*(1), 69–91.

CHAPTER 6

El Sacrificio de una Madre: A Mother's Sacrifice

Ana Bautista

In this poem, I briefly narrate my walk as a woman who endured domestic violence for more than two decades. More specifically, in this poem originally written in Spanish and translated into English, I expose my constant struggles to get ahead and the impasses I found along the way when I immigrated to the United States.

Dicen que la vida es simple,
solo hay que saberla vivir.
Pero cuando el golpe y
la desgracia no se suelta,
¿cómo hace para fluir?

They say life is simple,
you just have to know how to live.
But when life's blows and
misfortune do not release you,
How do you breathe?

Fueron años de desasosiego,
golpes, burlas, y desamor.
Pero la lucha por mis hijos,
dibujando sus sonrisas,
hacían de mis días un simple
borrador.

There were years of anxiety,
hitting, teasing, and heartbreak.
But fighting for my children,
drawing their smiles,
became the restart button of all
my days.

Un mortal de medio pelo,
sin promesas ni pudor,
con arraigo y cobardía,
día a día destruía,
con palabras y un gran pulso
de mi vida el albor.

A worthless mortal,
without promises or modesty,
day by day holding me back,
cowardly destroying,
with every word and beating,
my life's dawn.

Dos retoños me seguían,
por doquier en mi andar.
Y aún con golpes y tropiezos
simplemente esquivaba mi tristeza
y decidía simular

Two little ones followed me,
everywhere in my walk.
And even with bumps and stumbles
I just sidestepped my sadness
showing a smile for them.

© KONINKLIJKE BRILL NV, LEIDEN, 2021 | DOI: 10.1163/9789004446182_006

Todo esto se unía,
como pila de basura,
y como a pedir de boca
se juntaba a la fila
de mi país su azote y desventura.

Fui maestra por pasión.
Enseñar me refrescaba.
Las sonrisas y los juegos
de mis niños me abrazaban.

Siempre el nombre de maestra
lo llevaba con orgullo,
pues fui parte de mil vidas
que formé desde capullo.

Desde niños hasta jóvenes,
desfilaban en la pizarra.
Unos lentos otros prestos
con sapiencia o ignorancia
aprendían con constancia.

Yo lo puedo en esta vida
era la consigna de mi almohada
y por eso las arrugas,
el cansancio y las lágrimas
en mi cara se anclaban.

Muy temprano en la mañana,
mi jornada comenzaba,
hijos míos a la escuela,
y yo a la mía enseñaba.

En la tarde regresaba
me fundía en un abrazo
con anécdotas y besos
terminaba en mi regazo.

All of this came together,
like a pile of garbage,
and to top it all off
my country joined the line
with its scourge and misfortune.

I became a teacher out of passion.
Teaching was refreshing.
The smiles and the games
of my children were embracing.

Always the name of teacher
I wore it with pride,
after all, I was part of a thousand lives
that I formed from an early age.

From children to young people,
they paraded by the blackboard.
Some slow, others quick
wisely or ignorantly
they would learn constantly.

I can do it all in this life
became the motto of my pillow
and that is why the wrinkles,
tiredness and tears
became anchored in my face.

Very early in the morning
my journey would begin,
my children would go to their school,
and I would teach in mine.

In the afternoon I would return
and I would melt into a hug
with anecdotes and kisses
ending up on my lap.

Era ahí donde iniciaba
el infierno, en carne propia.
El mortal se sumergía
en alcohol y groserías.
¡Todos corran a sus cuartos!
Y juguemos al que no oía.

Golpe, engaño y sufrimiento
era toda su poesía,
pues su mente no alcanzaba
a ver cuánto su mujer valía.

Ya los días transcurrían,
era todo un reiterar;
en la mañana alegría,
en la noche a llorar.

Entre lágrimas y apuros
mi alma se debatía
en continuar mi pasión
a cambio de la destrucción.

La pobreza de mi pueblo
y una guerra que emergía.
El ardor de mi infierno,
solo penas padecía.

Con astucia y valentía,
hice todo por huir
de aquel hombre vil, cobarde,
de un pueblo en agonía,
y muchos años de combate.

Un adiós a mi familia,
dos luceros de mi mano,
un equipaje ligero,
y un llanto no en vano.

It was there where it started
a hell, in the flesh.
The mortal was submerged
in alcohol and profanity.
Everyone, run to your rooms!
And let's play pretending you don't
hear.

Beatings, deception, and suffering
it was all his poetry
because his mind could not fathom
the value of his woman.

The days would pass by,
it was quite a reiteration;
in the morning joy,
at night back to lamentation.

Between tears and troubles
my soul was struggling
to continue my passion
in exchange for destruction.

The poverty of my people
and a war that was emerging.
The burning of my hell,
only pain I suffered.

With ingenuity and courage,
I did everything to run away
of that vile, cowardly man,
of a town in agony,
and of many years of battles.

Goodbye to my family
two bright stars by my hand,
light luggage,
and a cry that was not in vain.

El horizonte se veía,
un mundo para ampliar
sin opción a regresar,
no quedó más que emigrar.

A un país desconocido
llegamos sin voltear
con la fuerza de un guerrero
y solo ganas de luchar.

Tranquilos hijos míos
no se apuren en su andar
que de aquí en adelante
Dios nos lleva a ganar.

Con tres pesos en la bolsa,
un estómago vacío,
el cuerpo lleno de miedo,
y de frente solo frío.

Ya salgamos de este túnel
hijos míos de mi amor
que de aquí en adelante
solo risas y primor.

No es fácil el comienzo.
Una vida enmendar
pero libre de ese averno
todo puede mejorar.

Con astucia se trabaja
y con ganas de triunfar
ya no hay tiza ni tablero
solo casas por limpiar.

Ese cargo de maestra
en mi alma siempre está
y no pierdo la esperanza
de volver a enseñar.

The horizon was visible,
a world to expand
with no option to return,
there was nothing left but to emigrate.

To an unknown country
we arrived without return,
with the strength of a warrior
and the will to fight nonstop.

Be calm, my children
do not rush in your walk
because from now on
God will lead us to triumph.

With three dollars in the bag,
an empty stomach,
my body full of fear,
and facing the cold.

Let's get out of this tunnel
my children, my loves
because from now on
there will only be laughter and joy.

The beginning is not easy.
It is not easy to mend a life,
but free from that hell
everything will be fine.

With ingenuity, you must work
and always wanting to succeed
there is no more chalk or board
only houses to be cleaned.

Being a teacher
is always in my soul
and I do not lose hope
to teach again one day.

Sometida a un papel,	Surrendered to a piece of paper,
Que de verde debe estar,	that must always be green,
sin medir la valentía,	without measuring bravery,
lucha, fuerza y bienestar.	fight, strength, and well-being.

Otro idioma hablan mis hijos.
Da gusto entender
con que ellos ya progresen
aunque yo no pueda ya crecer.

Another language my children speak.
It is nice to understand
that this is their time to advance
although I may no longer progress.

Soy creyente de la suerte
con o sin talento
los tropiezos e impases
simplemente los enfrento.

I am a believer of luck
with or without talent
stumbling blocks and impasses
I simply face what is to come.

Con esta estrofa me despido,
no sin antes recordar
que en los ojos del creador
nunca nos va a desamparar.

With this stanza I say goodbye,
not without first remembering
that in the eyes of the creator
we will never be forsaken.

I am a mother of three beautiful children, Nicolás, Ana María, and Evan and I am also a teacher by profession. I earned a master's degree in education in my native country of Colombia where I also taught for many years. Three years ago, we arrived in Atlanta, GA without knowing that I could not practice my profession here because I needed an additional document. All of these protocols were new to me and I did not know what steps I needed to take to return to the classroom and to teach here in the United States. Although I am not currently teaching, I do have to work to provide for our family. Every day I work in any job that comes my way, anything that becomes available. Nonetheless, I do not lose hope in returning to the classroom and continuing my career as a teacher in the United States. I believe dreams do not have an expiration date; we just need to take a deep breath and continue pushing forward until we reach our goals.

CHAPTER 7

Domestic Tongues

Mauricio Patrón Rivera

These words are about myself right now, on a moment I am trying to be with others in a new country and a new tongue. I am discovering the relationship that I have with this territory, I cannot be the same person here in a different country with a different language than the one I was in Mexico. I believe people belong to the landscape. In this poem, I explore this landscape in three different orbits, the inner one, the domestic one, and the university one. Here I ask myself about the one I used to be, my desires and the possibilities to be with others.

> Domestic was
> a CD I lost
> long time,
> long distance, ago.
>
> I hum the songs
> while I clean, even
> if the lyrics
> do not trespass
> to this new place.
>
> In the bayou city
> with my hands on the dishes,
> the soap repeats
> my thoughts
> in a different voice.
>
> I am a mopped
> wet line,
> linking two
> places,
> waiting to be dry.

and the songs are
coming. I long for them
but the city's dust
comes again and
I have to clean my way

to the present.
tengo un escarabajo escarbando mi pecho

lo tengo abrochado a mi clavícula
por una cadena y se mueve
entre mis pelos como un maquech
de brillos en el lomo.

en secreto le doy
las instrucciones para abrir
esta máquina deseante.

el maquech extrae piedras
negras minúsculas
me las da de comer.

la lengua la tengo partida
desde que sentí los afectos
dañada un parte la otra
viva a la mitad.

testigo de la podredumbre
de las palabras
con las que sé querer
el maquech me da más piedras.

I am two guys sitting in a bar
not knowing they like each other
there is something kinda cute about them
but all I can see is my own
double shadow.

the university's
most stressful
space is the hallway
of my department

she está
peliada:

with him
who was friends
with her

with her
who used to
collaborate with

he made his
own company
and took:

dear dean

she began a program
on writing and
community but
now writes about

I hope the air current in
your office is fresh but this
hallway isn't at the threshold
I was happy walking by
exchanging hellos from
door to door in the middle

her & her
with him.

stones.

I became anxious about
saying anything next to a
wrong door to have an
opinion outside the

she just got
a mental
breakdown

twenty
teacher assistants
share two rooms

classroom at the end I'm
just sad of walking this alley
with just some few nice

they failed
to fight for
better wages

everything seems
to be ok.

fellows it makes me think of
the other passages beyond

the email
became quiet.

he took a sabbatical
after being accused
of harassment.

this one in the english or
the art departments we
are divided in minorities
where I was thinking we
were divided by scientific
thought in two years of being
an immigrant student you

the professor who
presented the case
was herself
accused of
abuse of power.

she didn't have
enough students
to open her seminar,
last semester she was
accused of
discriminatory

already find the place for me
kind regards

comments.

cuando crucé esa puerta
me dormí al servicio
de otra casa que no era mía
la lengua se me hizo
orden al secarse
el río que traía
en la espalda.

sorri about the
carpet, I throw
the tongue there
and it started
to write the
broken words of
my story on
the carpet *sorri*.

I tighten up my frontier
to keep it tight is the warranty
of me being a man
I am afraid to loose it
and discharge on the State

in the geographies
the border of myself
is not a wall but
an abyss sealed by
the frighten flesh

I do not wanna loose
my warranty
become a nonrefundable guy
with a broken void
between the legs

porque estamos peliados
y si ya no soy de este lado
ya poco me garantiza
mi estado mafioso asignado
me quita la protección

y cómo hay un
yo sin estado

me reconozco como un damnificado
las relaciones sexogenéricas
aceptadas por la máquina
que llaman hombre no
aparecen en mi lista de deseos.

In this poem, the word "peliada" follows Anzaldúa's idea that "for people of color and other outsiders, the academy is a wounding field" (2015, p. 76). For some of us, who came to the United States to study, the university became our home and it is hard to realize that it is broken. How can we transform the university and our own places into safe spaces of learning and joy? I think about it while I scrub out my home and myself, changing the landscapes one stone at the time. I find out that my relationship with others is also my relationship with words, and I write for those who need the feeling of home. The domestic tongue is the one I use to speak and create safe spaces for me and the people I care about.

Reference

Anzaldúa, G. (2015). *Light in the dark/Luz en lo oscuro. Rewriting identity, spirituality, reality* (A. Keating, Ed.). Duke University Press.

CHAPTER 8

Mariposa: A Two-Part Poem

Zurisaray Espinosa

Part I

I burst with emotions
reading words into phrases
inside a maze, without a map.
I untangle my humanity.

An infant inside the body of a woman
pretending to understand,
head barely above water.

¡SOCORRO!
Me ahogo y trago toxinas.
Intento descargar—
una historia de abuso marginal
de mi identidad, clase social, y sexo.
Es un dolor impuesto que me deteriora por dentro.

Polluted waters inside of me
keep me leaking polluted thoughts,
drowning deep inside my ocean body,
My lungs plead for air.

Part II

Es que me gusta bañarme entre dos mundos,
evocando sentimientos escondidos,
me siento completa,
platónicamente sensual
taking risks with my keyboard
between ways of being.

© KONINKLIJKE BRILL NV, LEIDEN, 2021 | DOI: 10.1163/9789004446182_008

Me siento realizada,
embracing all parts of myself,
mi cuerpo de poca simetría
en todo su esplendor.

In constant flux
con mis pensamientos
hablándole al mundo
usando mi escritura.
No sabía que tenía cosas que decir.

¡Sí! "Soy cubana," sin duda.

I am Cuban indeed because people say that Cubans like to talk. I did not know I could talk like us, like Cubans, because I did not feel like one for a very long time. I was too busy trying to assimilate into contexts I thought would help me succeed in life. In this chapter, I thus offer parts of my *historia* in the hopes that others will continue to see themselves within the literature written by people of color in the U.S. context. I would like to ask, who are we residing at the margins and borders of metaphorical and literal worlds? We are the working-class people with accents that a mainstream-Eurocentric society ignores. I created this poem numb, unaware of what I was writing until I was done and tired of crying. I am an impostor within a world that ignores my spirit.

I am the daughter of Cuban immigrants. I did not reflect on my life experiences through an immigrant perspective until I moved to a place where people do not look or speak like me. When I first moved to Georgia, I worked in a kitchen and felt invisible as I struggled to finish a bachelor's degree that took six years to complete. For a very long time, I was voiceless, having escaped a situation from my past that kept me in a constant state of depression and anger. Now, I realize that my contextualized lived experiences were not my doing. My race, social class, and gender do not define, label, or box me into the stereotype people have of me. Now I scream and fight for my human rights. I want people to know that *I* exist. People have had prejudiced ideas of me because of the way I look, the jobs I have had, and the way I speak English with an accent. What is wrong with having an accent? I think it sounds exotic, or so I have been told.

My lungs do get a bit of fresh air every now and then when I write and create art. I have consciously suppressed my writing and artistic creativity for more than fifteen years now, but I will not do it anymore. I will re-frame where

I see myself in the future because I firmly believe we should all have space in our lives for reflection, creativity, and self-empowerment. People who are constantly trying to survive within the framework of hegemonic structures that work to defeat the human spirit, rather than enliven them, should have access to this creative and authentic way of being.

My adult self is realizing there is power in viewing the world through a critical lens. There is great power in speaking and writing after one is able to re-frame one's *historia*. The work becomes even more meaningful when one is able to continually revisit one's evolving identity. I have become accustomed to thinking deeply about my life, even though it often brings me (un)necessary pain. The pain is healing because I begin to understand that I am not alone in my experiences. It is true, even though I write this message of self-compassion, embracing all parts of myself has not been easy. The unresolved emotional traumas I experienced in my childhood and youth are still very present with me as an adult. I have yet to feel a sense of belonging in the world of academia. I have yet to come to terms that I am a construct of all my experiences and that I have to be enough for this world. I continue to work within myself as I figure out where I stand within the research I hope to undertake in the future. My future work will be the kind of research that empowers young Latina/o and Urban Youths to think critically, to act in the welfare of their own well-being, and to have positive life outlooks in order to accomplish their goals in the United States.

The art piece in Figure 8.1 is an extension of myself. I am seeking peace with my inner child and woman. The fetus in my lower abdomen is my unborn self. The woman's figure is a dark silhouette because I am still in the process of *becoming*. The sun behind me represents my growing knowledge of the small and the big truths. It is no coincidence I am sitting on top of the world. A feminist, I am a woman who believes in equality for all marginalized individuals. I have never liked the color red because red reveals my womanhood, PERIOD. I feel like a woman, but sometimes I feel like a man because I am envious of their indisputable rights. The woman would like more rights! Under the sun is a visible part of our glamorous moon which provides some shade from all the new knowledge I must endure. I extend my arms wide open to new experiences. I have been unplugged from the matrix, no longer confused, but anxious, very anxious about meeting the world for the very first time.

FIGURE 8.1   Becoming

CHAPTER 9

Beloved

Jamie Harris

"Beloved, let us love one another. For love is of God and everyone that loveth is born of God and knoweth God. He that loveth not, knoweth not God for God is love, so beloved, let us love one another" (I John 4:7-8, The New King James Version) is a song, from my youth in my birthplace, *Trinidad*, that plays in my head.

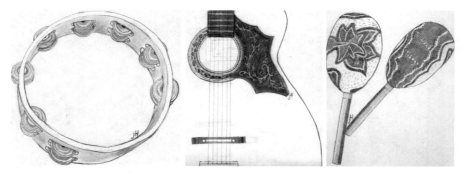

FIGURE 9.1   Sketches of three instruments: A tambourine, a guitar, and shak-shak

In my memory, this song is accompanied by the *tambourine* my mom would play while we sang hymns, by the strums of my dad's rhythm guitar, and by the voice of my little brother beside me.

"Beloved" is accompanied by the *shak-shak* that was so skillfully played by the Shak-Shak man, as I called him, who brought tears to my eyes when I would watch him play in the first row of seats at the village church; he was disabled in everyone's eyes, but very able in God's eyes.

"Beloved" hums every time I reach out and extend my hand to lift up colleagues who may not feel as though they belong—imposter syndrome, they call it—maybe because of her cultural norms, or her personality, or his lack of connections—I reach out to lift them up.

To be seen, speak, and be heard.

"Beloved" hums every time I reach out and extend my hand to lift up another who needs a new beginning—those who are a part of vulnerable populations—immigrants, human trafficked victims, and the illiterate. It is a calling that energizes me, teaching, helping, serving. It is not about vulnerability; it is about believing in that person's heritage, value, and strength. It is about equipping individuals, families, and communities to live freely and be empowered.

To be seen, speak, and be understood.

"Beloved" hums every time I reach out and extend my hand to lift up those who are left on the outside; those who do not belong. I see them. I seek them out. I offer them a way in. They do not need to return anything to me—they just need to be.

To be seen, speak, and be known.

"Beloved," the journey of our lives, good and bad, makes us who we are. I am because I experienced the neither-nor spaces and know what it is like to not belong. Born a Trinidadian and granted the privilege of more opportunities in the United States—to Trinidadians, I am American, and to Americans, I am Trinidadian. The neither-nor spaces. Where do I belong?

I belong to the beloved.

I now know that I have the beautiful privilege of being fully me—one with a beautiful blend of both. I am Trinidadian American. *Soca, Parang*, and *Calypso* mixed with classical, gospel, and jazz; *mangoes, guava,* and *plantain* blended with strawberries, blueberries, and peaches; World English melded with American Standard English; *Calaloo, Jalebe*, and *Sorrel* combined with turkey, apple pie, and lemonade. All a part of me—I have now accepted and know that I belong. That I am beloved.

"Beloved" hums every time.

Final Thoughts

The words of the song "Beloved" come from a Bible verse that has never left me all these years. It is a memory, one I remember from those early years in Trinidad and Tobago, my home. I came to the United States as a young child. While I have experienced success, there have been many adaptations and learnings along the way. As an adult, I have embraced my Trinidadian culture, but as a child and teenager, I just wanted to be as American as I could be. The truth is that I grew up in a Trinidadian household, so even now, as an adult, my extraordinary husband still teaches me things about American culture and language that I never knew.

In the poem, the sketches are of the actual instruments in my or my parents' possession, and italicized words represent things from Trinidad that I still enjoy. I still enjoy conversations with my grandmothers over the phone and hold tightly to those things from my origin that I can still touch and feel. I am grateful for them—I am grateful that it was not too late to hold on and not let go. These are things I hope to share with my own children, so they know the beautiful diversity within them—my beloved.

PART 2

Personal Narratives

∴

CHAPTER 10

Subtle Bangla Traits

Ben Haseen

When I was brought into this world, I was not the only one looking up at her. I had a partner. That partner was my beloved sister who came into this world with me. She has been with me since I took my first breath, the first time light peeked into my eyes, and the first time I uttered the words "Mommy!" People always tell me that I am lucky to have a twin sister, and a huge part of me is incredibly grateful to have her in my life. However, people do not realize the struggles that twins must go through growing up in Bangladesh where healthcare is limited.

My mother received limited prenatal care. When people looked at both my sister and me, we looked like happy young toddlers, but my sister did not start uttering words until long after most kids begin speaking in small sentences. When she would reach out to grab things, you would notice her hand tremor. You would notice how hard it was for her to catch balls because her movements were not fast enough. They were just little things that would not matter to the average person, but my sister's struggles with having to adapt to a country where the disabled are often stripped away from opportunity became the catalyst for the rest of my and my younger brother's lives.

When my brother was born, my sister and I were very excited. We were happy three-year-olds welcoming a new life into our family. My brother was loved and pampered by everyone. Meanwhile, my father was gone most of the time in a foreign land called America, and my sister and I were just starting preschool. Life seemed very tranquil during those times. But a lot of it was masked by the ignorance of the truths that existed, the truths that we were unaware of in Bangladesh because we were in the bubble of living with a family that sheltered us until we reached school-going age. It was a new change in the direction of how our family ran.

Going to an English School in Dhaka

My grandfather lived a very privileged life in Dhaka, the capital of Bangladesh; he had a business that allowed him to support his entire family. So, when it was time for us to start going to preschool, my grandfather enrolled my sister

© KONINKLIJKE BRILL NV, LEIDEN, 2021 | DOI: 10.1163/9789004446182_010

and me into an English-only private school. I was too young to realize what my grandfather had done, stripping us from the opportunity to learn Bangla, the language of our country, and our culture. My parents were provided the comfort that we would learn our language at home and learn English, a symbol of intellect and prosperity, at school.

The entire school curriculum was in English. We had a Bangla writing class that I hardly remember because almost all my other classes had me reading texts in English. Instead of reading about the history of how Bangladesh came to be, and the bloodshed that took place so that the people of Bangladesh could have the freedom to speak Bangla, my teachers thrust me into reading "The Three Billy Goats Gruff" and "Stone Soup."

In fact, the only reference to the culture of our country that this school embraced was our forest green uniforms that mimicked the national flag. But it still ignored the dark red circle in the middle of the flag. The dark red circle signifies the blood spilled to protect our nation's language, culture, and people. The reason Bangladesh decided to become its own country was because its people were being silenced from speaking their native tongue. It was as if entering this school was stripping away the history that my ancestors fought for.

Despite being required to read tales that I could not relate to, I excelled in school. I reveled in wanting to know more and being considered intelligent by my teachers. Even though teachers expected me to know the experiences of those living in Western cultures which I never had any relation to, I had a strong desire to excel. My sister, on the other hand, struggled incredibly. She was often chastised by teachers for falling behind and not being able to catch up with the other students. I remember that teachers would be unfairly cruel because when she frustrated them, they would hit her in the hand with a ruler. I remember letting my sister look at my assignments so that she could perform better in the limited time we were given to study. I did my best as a sibling to be there for her, but eventually, unknown to my knowledge, it would not be enough.

Going to the United States

By the time we were ready to enroll in elementary school, my mother received some very sad news from the school administration. They were refusing to admit my sister because they feared that she would not be able to keep up with the material. They told my mother that they had no other options for my sister and that maybe it would be best for her to just stay home. My mother tearfully refused to allow that to happen. She saw, before anyone, the potential my sister had to influence those around her. My mother saw the potential the administration at the English school refused to see in my sister, refusing to give her any source of accommodations to support her success. My mother immediately contacted my father and within a few months, my brother, sister, and I were on our first plane trip ever, headed to the United States of America.

Going to Elementary School in the US

Starting elementary school was a scary endeavor. I started elementary school in the United States in 2002, one year after the September 11 attacks on the World Trade Center. At the time, there were a lot of anti-Islamic sentiments that reinforced hostility against Muslims living in America. We had to walk to school and young men would approach my mother to ask her "why are you here?" with aggression and anger. My mother, who could not understand English at the time, had a very traumatic experience attempting to protect herself and her children. Like my mother, I feared whether my communication skills were good enough; was I going to get bullied by my classmates, too? I remember being absolutely terrified of having to speak up in class.

Luckily, my first-grade teacher, Mr. Gutierrez, who was Latinx, understood my struggle of having to assimilate to this new culture that I was thrust into. He allowed a nurturing environment for me to feel comfortable to speak up, practice the English that I had learned in preschool, and build on it. He bought and gifted me books and comics to read so that I could learn to adjust by not only improving my reading comprehension but also heavily centering around American culture so that I could learn to adapt. After a few weeks, the school faculty reached out to me and my siblings' teachers and asked whether we should be enrolled in the English as a second language (ESL) program that many immigrant children have to go through as a rite of passage to feel accepted in America.

Mr. Gutierrez absolutely refused to place me in ESL. He believed in me, and he understood that ESL sometimes does more harm than good to immigrant students. It makes students like me, my sister, and my brother feel alienated. I remember that ESL students would often get teased about having to be placed in another class. I saw fluent English-speaking students make derogatory remarks against students in ESL, often judging their level of intelligence. I believe ESL is a program that, although has good intentions, can lead to students feeling like their own culture is the fault of their misery. As a consequence, some ESL students begin to reject their own cultures and start to change who they are, so they are accepted. My brother and sister, unfortunately, went through that exact same instance. While my sister benefited greatly from physical therapy, being placed in the ESL program awakened a new sense of insecurity within her.

She began to adopt American customs by choosing to emulate the girls and women she would see in teen shows. She developed a fascination with pop music and shows like Hannah Montana that put a great emphasis on trendy looks and the necessity of buying things. Eventually, my sister went from speaking Bangla to speaking limited Bangla, to forgetting almost all of it. My brother also went through a similar crisis. He completely adopted English over Bangla refusing to speak Bangla as much as possible. He distanced himself from our parents, opting instead to socialize with his English-speaking friends from school. Over time he lost his ability to speak our language as well. To this day he has no desire to speak or learn it. My siblings began to subconsciously blame our immigrant identity for the problems they faced in school, and the fear of not being wanted by our classmates. They found their escape through emulation of the characteristics they believed would allow them to fit in.

At the time I was too young to realize what was happening and I too felt the strong desire to be wanted and desired by classmates. Like my siblings, I started to involve myself in what my classmates were doing. I told myself that Santa was real even though I found it weird that a peculiar white man was delivering gifts all over the world. Why did I not ever receive any of Santa's gifts? I remember being very aware of how I was changing myself but never pondered to stop and think. It was not until I reached adulthood that I realized how my siblings and I were socialized as children. Maybe it is because as children we see the world through a non-self reflective lens and our primary desires are belongingness and love with others. Usually, these characteristics in children allow them to become more sociable and compassionate. However, because there was a disruption in our childhood when we moved to the States and the feelings of alienation from our peers, we used these innate childhood behaviors to change our identity instead of giving our identities more depth.

Going into the Present

Years later as the three of us hit our early 20's, much has changed about how much we hold on to the language our ancestors fought for. My sister, over time, has unlearned many of the false realities she was forced to adopt as a new immigrant. Even though she has lost much of her fluency, she still attempts to maintain what she has left of Bangla. She engages in dialogue with my mother every day to keep what she has left strong. Even my mother has noted that her Bangla has started to falter after being here for more than 15 years. My brother, unfortunately, has released himself from having the burden of not knowing his native tongue. He has become content with communicating only in English, even though every time our grandparents call, he is unable to communicate with them. I do not blame my brother. Having to relearn something so inherent to our upbringing is hard and can retrigger the traumas that we went through. It is also why my sister does not go through the effort of taking Bangla classes because, at this point, it is something that will make us relive the struggles that we first went through when we came to the States.

Finally, I begin to look at myself. How has my relationship with my native language changed over time? Did having to go through elementary school without the stress of ESL change the way I perceived being bilingual? When I look back, I am incredibly grateful to have the love that I received from my first-grade teacher, Mr. Gutierrez. He believed in me, and his trust allowed me to not just become assimilated to American culture, but also to hold on to Bangla. Instead of signing me into the ESL program soon after starting class, he practiced patience. He took time to see if I was able to grasp English and communicate with my classmates when participating in our classroom activities. When I would have trouble coming up with what to say, he would wait until I found the right string of words. He took the time to conclude that I was capable of understanding and speaking English with in-class activities instead of a formal ESL program. He was a teacher that knew children are capable of learning very quickly because their brains are better at adapting to new situations than adults'.

I can still speak conversational Bangla, even though my vocabulary is slipping as the years go by because I hardly ever have the chance to speak it. What is more fascinating is that growing up, I felt most outcasted by my Bangla community as I came to understand that I was queer. While my brother and sister were able to express themselves more liberally in Bangladeshi-American spaces, I felt rejected and unloved which led me to reject my culture for years. Yet somehow, because of my positive experiences in elementary school, I still held on to my native language.

My brother, sister, and I are the products of young immigrants coming to the United States. We represent an identity that is in a halfway point that will never shift to one side or the other. We will never be perceived as true Americans because we were not born here but, at the same time, we are not Bangla either. If all three of us were to go back, we would be seen as "other" in the country that we were born in. We have lost most of the traits that made us Bangladeshi. We are just three people with subtle Bangla traits.

I plan on learning more about my culture and in turn learning more about myself. In the last year, I met a large group of South Asian and Bangladeshi advocates who have the same passions I do and, with them, I can practice not just my Bangla, but also recreate the relationships that I had with my culture before I began to fade away from it. I found a community to call home and accept my dual identities. A community that embraces those identities and challenges me to contribute to making this country a welcoming place for all people. Lastly, with these new connections, I can learn to love my dual identities and embrace my imperfections as something that does not need to be changed.

CHAPTER 11

You Had Better Turn off the Fan: Communicative Competence in Practice

Jiyoon Lee

Arrival

It was one late August morning in 1999 when I landed in Detroit, MI. On the day I arrived in the United States, I learned that my connecting flight from Detroit to Harrisburg, PA had been canceled due to a storm. Before I came to the United States, I was confident enough to decide to study at an American college as an exchange student for a year. This confidence came from my extensive English language studies at a prestigious foreign language high school and at a respectful college in South Korea. At my high school, students had their major and minor languages; mine were German and Mandarin Chinese, respectively. Everyone in South Korea studies English as a mandatory academic subject from a young age. About half of my high-school course work consisted of English, German, and Mandarin Chinese, including four hours a week of speaking classes with native speakers of English and German. In English classes, differing from other local high schools, we read English newspaper articles, reports, and novels. We also wrote short responses and essays. In English-speaking class, we acted, made presentations, and participated in discussions and debates. My major at college was English language and literature. I read 18th, 19th, and 20th century British and American novels written in English, made presentations in English, wrote essays and reports in English, and studied the English language and linguistics extensively. However, I found that what I had learned at schools in South Korea did not help me too much during the crisis at the Detroit airport.

Upon my arrival, I felt completely overwhelmed. It was such an exhausting experience trying to figure out my current situation and what would happen to my trip. After several cancellations of flights and rearrangements, it was already midnight when I arrived at the Harrisburg, PA airport. Gratefully, two staff members from the college where I would stay for a year came to pick me up. Soon after we got on the road, I started feeling worried that I might have been taken to the wrong place. The highway that I could see through the car windows was pitch-black, surprising for a person who came from a megalopolitan city like Seoul, South Korea, where streets and roads are always well lit. But I was too tired to think further about it. About an hour later, we arrived at a small women's college in rural Pennsylvania. I was taken to the dorm room where I would stay for a year. It was a freshman dorm: a small room with two beds, desks, closets, and shelves in parallel positions. I selected one side and crashed into bed. The next morning, I went outside to find that I was in the middle of nowhere. I could not hear much around me except for birds, and I could not see much except for a few two- or three-story school buildings and endless lawn. A few days later, the incoming freshmen arrived, my roommate was among them.

First Encounter

When my roommate walked into the room, I could read the shock on her face when she saw me, *a foreigner.* She was a Caucasian girl from a small town in rural Pennsylvania. Later I learned that growing up, she had rarely met people of color, not to mention a person from another country. Similar to my roommate, I was experiencing many feelings. I remember asking myself different questions like "How can I stay with someone I have never met in this small room for a year?", "Do I speak English with her all the time?", "Are we going to get along?". After a brief introduction, we went to a series of freshmen orientations and events. After a long day, we were ready for bed. It was truly awkward to share a tiny room with someone I had just met a half day ago. We said good night and turned off the light. My roommate then turned on her electric fan! I started to worry so much that I decided to advise her about the fan. I constructed a grammatically perfect sentence in my mind and said, "you had better turn off the fan."

Fan Death

There was a brief but awkward silence. Then, my roommate replied, "why?" in a defiant tone. Why? *Why* is the question that makes second language learners stumble, which usually requires more elaborate explanations with more vocabulary and grammar to respond. I was thus puzzled by her question. In my culture, it is *common sense* for people to turn off electric fans when they sleep. Growing up in South Korea, I remember watching a news report about a death caused by an electric fan in the summer due to hypothermia or suffocation. I found out later that what was common sense among Koreans even made a Wikipedia entry; it was addressed in a New York Times article in 2016 and shared in NBC news in 2018. Does it mean it is not common sense?

The interaction happened in a time before we could use a smartphone or do a quick Google search. I tried to explain the dangers of leaving on an electric fan while sleeping to my roommate who had never been exposed to a different culture and had never met a person who did not speak English as their first language until she met me in 1999. After hearing my stumbling common-sense explanation, she said, "it does not make any sense." It was the end of the story. She went to bed with the fan on. First, I was embarrassed to realize that my English explanation was not clear enough to persuade her. Then, I tried to hear her breathing through the night, hoping that I did not find a dead body the following morning. It was almost dawn when I fell asleep. The riddle of that night's interaction stayed with me for a long time. Despite the awkward first encounter with her, we have continued our friendship.

Seeking Graduate Education

After a year at the American college, I went back to my college in South Korea. Finishing my senior year there, just like many senior students, I tried to figure out what I would do next. Fortunately, I had a few options. Because I became a certified teacher upon graduation from my college, I could pursue a full-time English teaching position at a secondary school in South Korea. My parents were also willing to support me so I could attend graduate school to pursue a master's degree in a field that I developed an interest in during my college years. A third option was to get a job at a company where they valued good English skills, like many of my friends did. Among all the options, I decided to pursue graduate education in a field that I studied at college and that I found most fascinating: *educational linguistics*. The field of educational linguistics centers on discussing the topics related to people's second language learning.

After talking to my professors and family members, I decided to apply to a graduate school in the U.S. instead of in South Korea. Applying to a school abroad requires extensive preparation. I needed to prepare a statement of purpose, undergraduate grade point average (GPA), test of English as a foreign language (TOEFL) score, graduate record examination (GRE) score, and had to translate to English and notarize all relevant documents. I submitted my application in winter 2000 and received admissions from three universities in spring 2001. I decided to go to the University of Pennsylvania, also known as Penn.

Pursuing a master's degree in teaching English to speakers of other languages (TESOL) at Penn was a challenging experience. The number of readings and depth of knowledge required at Penn was not comparable to my previous experiences in college. For every class, I had much to read. Sometimes, professors assigned an entire book for a week's reading requirement along with several research articles. Each course also required extensive writing, oral presentations, and in-class discussions. Before starting graduate work, I was only concerned about my pronunciation and academic speaking ability; however, pursuing a graduate degree was much beyond it. Looking back to those years, I can now attest that being proficient in reading and writing in a second language was the key to my success in academia.

Theoretical Explanation

While I was pursuing a master's degree at Penn, I finally got the answer to the riddle I could not solve earlier: the riddle of my perfectly-developed grammatical sentence and its malfunction when I talked to my roommate in 1999. In one of the second language learning theory courses, I learned the concept of communicative competence (Canale & Swain, 1980). The theory of communicative competence says that knowing a language entails more than knowing its grammar well. The sentence, 'you had better turn off the fan' is a grammatically accurate sentence. The *Oxford English Dictionary* explains that you can use the past subjunctive of have (i.e., had) with adjectives or adverbs in the comparative (i.e., better) or superlative forms (i.e., best), and the expression requires a verb infinitive form coming after the word *better*. The grammatically accurate form is:

You had better + a verb in the infinitive form

It also explains that the expression can be used to express a speaker's preference or desirability or to tell the hearer about what the speaker thinks the hearer should do. However, the Oxford English Dictionary did not clearly explain when and with whom you can use the expression.

Canale and Swain (1980) argue that one's language ability is composed of four competencies including linguistic, sociolinguistic, discourse, and strategic competence. *Linguistic competence* refers to a language user's knowledge of vocabulary and grammar and the ability to process and produce grammatically accurate expressions. On the other hand, *sociolinguistic competence* refers to one's ability to use language appropriately per context. Those who have advanced sociolinguistic competence understand and use the appropriate expressions per context (e.g., a speaker-listener relationship, a listener's age, status, gender), the social distance between speakers and listeners, polite forms, nonverbal expressions, and cultural references. *Discourse competence* means that a language user's abilities to understand and produce the main points and organization, develop a conversation cohesively, and contribute to it accordingly. Finally, *strategic competence* refers to a language user's ability to use verbal and nonverbal strategies and manage communication breakdown.

This theory helped me understand that my knowledge of English grammar (i.e., linguistic competence) of composing a grammatically accurate sentence, 'you had better turn off the fan', was not enough to use English appropriately. I needed to understand that people do not use this expression with those whom they just met. I did not have enough understanding of social norms (i.e., sociolinguistic competence). I also did not have enough strategies (i.e., strategic competence) to mend the communication breakdown when my roommate asked me the reason why I said the expression, as well as after she said, 'that does not make any sense'.

The experience of studying my language uses and finding answers from research studies and established theories helped me develop more empathetic as well as critical perspectives of language learning and teaching. That is, it is possible to experience that sometimes those who speak English as their second language may unintentionally use some expressions that could be offensive or inappropriate. When hearing such expressions, before assuming that the speaker is rude or impolite, it is advisable to give another chance to them to clarify or elaborate on what they intended. It could be very possible that the person tried to convey something very meaningful but did not know the appropriate expressions for the context.

Teacher Education

My language learning journey continued when I was in a doctoral program. At those times, studying language learning theories had helped me explain my language use to those who were not familiar with non-native speakers' language use. After earning a Ph.D. in Educational Linguistics, I became a language testing researcher and a teacher educator. In my profession, I work with preservice language teachers who are studying in a language teacher-education program to obtain teaching credentials at schools and language centers in the U.S. and abroad (Lee, 2019).

Teaching an introductory linguistics course for preservice teachers, I have shared this story with them when explaining different aspects of language competence, emphasizing the diverse aspects of language learning and language use. I have observed that first, my students laugh at the story of fan death and then usually search for the concept on Google. I share this story with my students so that they are able to understand that knowing a language is a complicated concept like the concept of communicative competence. Some of them remember their own experience of making mistakes in foreign languages and share what their students had said to them. Finally, they develop further understanding and come up with ways to work with those who unintentionally use impolite or inappropriate expressions. While working with preservice teachers, I try to convey the idea that teaching a language entails not only knowing linguistic rules but also understanding the whole culture and people. After all, I believe that the purposes of learning a language are to communicate with people, understand the target culture in multiple ways, and become contributing members of society.

References

Canale, M., & Swain, M. (1980). Theoretical bases of communicative approaches to second language teaching and testing. *Applied Linguistics, 1*, 1–47.

Lee, J. (2019). A training project to develop teachers' assessment literacy. In E. White & T. Delaney (Eds.), *Handbook of research on assessment literacy and teacher-made testing in the language classroom* (pp. 58–80). IGI Global.

CHAPTER 12

Como una Leona: Shielding My Son from Discrimination at School

Aracelis Nieves

The first time I heard the phrase *Where there is a will, there is a way* I was in seventh grade and my English teacher mentioned it. I do not remember why my teacher taught us this phrase, but she did explain to us that if we fought and worked hard—if we persevered—we could achieve our dreams. I heard the same advice many times from my parents, my grandmother, my aunts, other teachers, our priest...

Another trendy phrase I remember from that time was that *education was the vehicle to improve your quality of life and your social class.* Although I did not understand what this meant, I did understand when my father used to say to me: *Nena, tú tienes que estudiar fuerte y obtener un diploma de la universidad porque si tu marido te sale un sinvergüenza, le das tres patadas* (Munchkin, you must study hard and earn a college degree, because if your future husband turns out to be a scoundrel you can kick him out of the house with no remorse). These lessons were my guide during my developmental years, and I think they guided me well. I can affirm that I have achieved almost all my dreams. Therefore, I tried to instill in my children this same way of thinking. Unfortunately, the world they were growing up in and the people around them were different. We no longer lived on a small island with a homogeneous Spanish-speaking population. Sadly, little by little I discovered that these ideologies did not apply to my children.

Trusting that education is the vehicle for social advancement, in 1992 I moved to the United States to continue my doctoral studies in education. My oldest son was ten years old; my daughter was four, and the youngest was just one year old. Everyone—except the baby, of course—was very excited; it was a great adventure. Eventually, all my children were enrolled at the same elementary school. This school was part of the university I was studying at, which had a prestigious school of education. The student population at this university (around 40, 000 students) was very diverse and most of the graduate students' children attended this elementary school; so, I thought my children would be safe there, free of prejudices, but I was wrong.

My Son's Blood Is Red, Too

I do not remember the exact moment when this happened, but I remember it was 1996 and Diego, my youngest son, was in kindergarten. It was around 3:00 pm and I was preparing after-school snacks for Angela, my daughter, and him when the phone rang. It was Diego's teacher telling me that Diego was suspended from school because he had a fight and, worst of all, the other student was hurt. When I asked if anything happened to my son, she responded that I did not have to worry; that he was ok and on the school bus on his way home. Fifteen minutes passed, but it felt like an eternity for me. I tried to remain calm while waiting for the school bus. When the bus arrived, we walked home. I served them snacks and waited until they finished eating so I could ask Diego his version of the incident. *We were returning from recess and I was singing while walking to the classroom,* he began narrating. *The boy in front of me told me to shut up; I asked him why and he responded because...* And then, what happened, I asked. *I continued singing, and he turned back and hit me on my face with his lunch box.* What did you do? I inquired. *I pushed him, he fell and got hurt with a desk.* Was he bleeding? I asked. *Yes, and me, too; but the teacher sent him to the nurse's office and cleaned my nose with a paper towel.* Were you bleeding? Did she not send you to the nurse's office as well? I screamed hysterically. My husband was still at work, but I called him and told him what happened. He immediately called the school and requested a meeting.

We met with the principal and the teacher the next morning. The teacher summarized her version of the incident and obviously, she forgot to comment that even though Diego was also bleeding, she did not send him to the nurse. The principal continued the conversation and alerted us that Diego did not have the social skills necessary to go to first grade; therefore, were planning on holding him in kindergarten, or so she thought.

Since I was very nervous, I could not think in English accurately; therefore, I started speaking in Spanish and asked my husband to translate. "Did you know that the other child attacked Diego first and my son only defended him-self?" "Did you know that my son had a bloody nose, but the teacher only sent the other student to the nurse's office?" I asked myself who was she to make that kind of decision? The pain and anger I felt increased with each question I asked. At the same time, I was thinking, how can they be so cruel to a five years old child? "My son has the same rights as the other kid. I wondered if she did not send Diego because he is Latino, and she inferred that he was responsi-ble for the incident when he was the victim. My son's blood is red, too!" There are no words to express the suffering, anger, and despair I was experiencing at that moment, only someone who has children can really know and understand that feeling.

The principal did not hide her consternation and her reproachful look towards the teacher. But I was not done. I told her that I was very sorry, but my son would go to first grade because I knew he mastered all the language and math skills taught up to that point. In addition, it was very sad that the academic year was ending, and we never had received any single note about Diego's accomplishments and good behavior. Apparently, she thought I did not know what I was talking about and she dared to ask me what skills I was referring to. I just responded, "I am completing a doctoral degree in curriculum and language education; I have been a teacher for many years; thus, I know what I am talking about." Unfortunately, I had to be as arrogant and pedantic as I could possibly be. Consequently, Diego was never suspended, the school administration apologized, and we received a note from the teacher celebrating Diego's accomplishments every week for the rest of the academic year.

Upon reflecting on this incident, I wondered how many parents were unable to protect or defend their children from incidents like these, and I wondered how many of these students ended up dropping out of schools after years of such forms of injustices. Latino students represent an estimated 26% of high school and elementary students across the country, and as a fast-growing demographic, are predicted to represent 30% of the nation by 2050 equivalent to 132 million students. Currently, one-in-four public elementary school students are Latinos. The percentage of kindergarten students of Latino descent increased from 14.9 percent in 1996, when my son was in first grade, to 25.7% in 2016 (Bauman, 2017). This is an indication that the young Latino population is growing quickly. According to the National Center for Education Statistics (NCES, 2019), in 2017 only 80% of Latino students graduated from high school compared to 91% of Asian Americans, 89% of Whites, 78% of African Americans, and 72% Native Americans.

Research conducted on Latino students has discovered several challenges affecting their education. One of those challenges is the mechanisms of discipline (Espinoza-Herold, 2003). The mechanisms practiced in schools cause Latino students' withdrawal because they feel that they are viewed as reckless and deceitful. Moreover, these practices are selectively enforced when Latino students are implicated. The data gathered by Espinoza-Herold (2003) regarding suspensions revealed that "given two schools with almost the same student enrollment, the urban institution with a majority Latino population had almost four times the number of suspensions than the institution with a majority White population" (Espinoza-Herold, 2003, p.124). Even though the researcher interviewed high school students, these mechanisms apparently start as soon as Latino students enter kindergarten, like what happened to my son.

A similar incident involving a fight occurred when Diego was in fourth grade in another collegiate city school in the same state. In this case, the principal was aware that my son just defended himself. However, she held us responsible for not teaching our son to seek an adult's help instead of fighting back and they wanted to suspend him because of that. We told her that, given the fact of past bullying experiences at school, we have told him to defend himself when and if he needs to. The principal did not say anything in that respect; the meeting just ended, and of course, Diego was not suspended.

Attention Deficit or Kinesthetic Intelligence?

It was the middle of October 1999, and like every year, we went to our first parent-teacher meeting at the school, where both my daughter Angela (sixth grade), and Diego (third grade) were attending. We did not want to waste time, so we decided that Victor, my husband, would go to Angela's classroom and I would go to Diego's. The meetings were with each parent individually and lasted about fifteen to twenty minutes. While I was waiting for my turn, I looked at Diego's works displayed on his desk, and also at what the teacher had posted in the classroom. On one of the walls, there was a chart in which she had identified her students' three strongest intelligences according to Howard Gardner's theory. I noticed that what the teacher had penciled in for Diego matched what I had already observed in him.

The teacher knew me because she taught my daughter in third grade as well; she even knew that I was studying my doctorate in education and that my husband was also studying his master's degree in adapted physical education. The first thing she mentioned after greeting me and after asking about "her favorite student Angela" was how different Angela and Diego were; "they are two extremes! She (Angela) is quiet, calm, disciplined, all goodness and sweetness; however, Diego…(and took a deep breath) he's pure dynamite!" This conversation started badly, I thought, but I just smiled and kept listening to her beautiful description of my beloved Boom Boom, as we affectionately nicknamed him…you can imagine why. Anyway, she was not saying anything that we did not know already; both were like that and as a mother, I had to accept it. The teacher's mistake was what she said next: "Therefore, Mrs. Nieves, we believe that Diego has attention deficit hyperactivity disorder. If you wish, we can recommend a specialist to certify it."

As we say in Puerto Rico: "Aquí fue donde la puerca entorchó el rabo" (*This is where the pig twisted the tail*—literal translation for a Puerto Rican colloquialism meaning "here is when the conversation turned wrong"). I reacted like a lioness defending her cubs. "Excuse me," I replied. As a teacher, I have the same training and knowledge you have on attention deficit; therefore, I am sure as an educator and as a mother, that my son does not suffer from that condition.

She was stunned; she was not expecting that reaction from me. I got up immediately and headed for the poster and she followed me like a robot. I pointed to my son's name and commented: "I have observed that you already know that Diego's strongest intelligences are kinesthetic, musical, and interpersonal. That means that he learns through movement, listening to music, and interacting with his classmates." The teacher just nodded. I continued saying, "then, I ask you, what activities do you include in your daily lesson plans to meet the needs of my son and everyone who is like him? If you only incorporate activities where students are sitting for more than twenty minutes, of course, they will get bored and look for something more interesting to do." The teacher had no choice but to rip up the appointment she had made with the psychologist. That was the end of our conversation, but not of the subject.

Two weeks had gone by and I attended a meeting of the *Women in Connection*. This was a support group for Latino mothers in which we discussed issues that impacted our families. Undoubtedly, I told them everything that had happened in my parent-teacher conference and, to my surprise, I uncovered a Pandora's Box. I could not believe several of the mothers who were there had been given an appointment with a psychologist for the same reason Diego's teacher tried to give me one. Their children attended the same school as mine. Realizing this "coincidence," we decided to explore in this meeting the question *How is it possible that all Latino students in that school have attention deficit and hyperactivity disorder?* After discussing the issue for a while, we concluded that perhaps they wanted to keep our children as zombies in the classroom since, at that time, they were prescribing Ritalin for that condition.

Supposedly, Ritalin helped increase students' ability to pay attention, stay focused on an activity, and control behavioral problems. It might have also helped the students in becoming organized and maybe improve their listening skills. However, in June 2005, the U.S. Food and Drug Administration issued a series of public health advisories warning that Ritalin and drugs like it, may cause visual hallucinations, suicidal thoughts, and psychotic behavior, as well as aggression or violent behavior.

Reflecting on this experience, I pondered how many students, now adults, have developed any of these conditions as a result of taking that medicine.

This incident took place in 1999 and, as a mother, I did not know much about this drug but, as a teacher, I had observed how medicated students behaved differently from their normal behavior. Instead of paying attention, students taking this drug daydreamed; they were physically in the classroom, but their thoughts were elsewhere. Therefore, teachers did not have to deal with them and worry about including different strategies or activities in the classroom to fulfill Latino students' learning needs. Several of these children did not speak English and needed additional help. In our meeting, we also asked ourselves, is this the new way to discriminate against minorities, especially against Latinos? All the mothers with a doctor's appointment for their children went to the school the following week and demanded an explanation from the school administration for that kind of tendency. As a result, no student was officially labeled with that condition.

My Son Is Not Going Anywhere

It was 2006 and now we were living in the wild and wonderful state of West Virginia. Diego was in tenth grade and he was playing with the junior varsity basketball team. My husband and I used to watch every single game, but that night we could not go. We were just arriving home from our schools' teacher-parent conferences when my husband received a call from one of the team's parents. His son had called him to tell him what had happened to Diego. Then, we received another call, and another and another, but none of them was our son. We texted him, even though we knew he was not allowed to use his cellphone when playing a game. I was desperate to hear Diego's version of the incident. We finally found out when the game was over and he was able to call us.

Apparently when they were driving to the game, one of the players said something inappropriate and the assistant coach heard it. The assistant coach asked who was to blame for those words and some players blamed Diego. Immediately, the assistant coach complained to my son but Diego replied stating he did not know what the assistant coach was talking about since he was playing on his cell phone. I will never forget the assistant coach's words toward my son, Diego...*"Go back to your country, we don't do that shit here in the United States."* Just remembering those words still breaks my heart. My husband and I did not know what to do, and then it occurred to me to call my supervisor, and my husband called a colleague to ask for advice.

That night we could not sleep; nevertheless, we arrived at Diego's school first thing in the morning. The principal was not there, so the assistant principal received us. We explained the reason for our visit and he immediately called the athletic director. Apparently, none of them knew what had happened. We introduced ourselves again, but this time emphasizing that we were both teachers and that, therefore, we were familiar with the protocol to follow in these cases. I also made sure they knew I had a doctorate degree in education. It may sound arrogant from my part, but sadly, we had already grasped that for many people in the United States, Latinos are nothing more than undocumented and illiterate individuals. My husband summarized what happened according to Diego and to the parents that called us. They were in shock; they knew they had everything to lose. They asked us what we wanted them to do. We demanded an apology from the assistant coach to Diego in front of the entire team; to humble himself in the same way he had humiliated our son. Both the assistant principal and the athletic director apologized and assured us that the assistant coach would apologize for his actions the very next day after basketball practice.

I could not go to the practice that Tuesday since I had to teach at night at the university, but my husband attended. We already imagined what would happen and we were prepared. The assistant coach apologized to the team in a very general way without specifying what he had done, and he did not apologize to Diego. When my husband left the practice, he was furious. The athletic director met my husband in the hallway. He asked my husband what was wrong and if he was not satisfied with the apology. My husband replied that if the assistant coach did not offer a sincere apology as we had demanded, both the coach and he would lose their jobs. My son's dignity was restored the next day.

The high school Diego attended consisted predominantly of White students and there were only 10 Latino students attending that institution. Diego was one of the only two Latino students playing in that team because he excelled in academics and was a very talented player. Diego was the shooting guard and the other Latino player was the point guard. Thanks to them, the following year, the team made it to the state championship for the first time in the school's history. I wonder if Diego would have had the opportunity of continuing playing basketball in the varsity team and of receiving a sports scholarship if we would not have defended him from that racial microaggression.

Unfortunately, not many Latino students can play in a state championship game, or even participate in a sports team. Although time has passed since my son's story, Latino students continue to be discriminated against in sports. For example, Latino students are not afforded the same opportunities, resources, and support students from other races receive. Such racial isolation in all educational disciplines including sports has detrimental effects on Latino students. In 2018, a civil rights advocacy group, the New York Lawyers for the

Public Interest, filed a class-action lawsuit, representing the student-led organization Integrate NYC Black and Latino students that were denied access to New York City public high school sports. According to this group, 17,000 New York City Black and Latino public high school students do not have any sports teams at their schools. They stated that:

> On average, Black and Latino students have access to far fewer teams and sports, and the city spends much less per Black and Latino students than for students of other races. Thousands of Black and Latino New York City public high school students attend schools that offer no team sports whatsoever, and Black and Latino students are twice as likely as students of other races to attend schools without sports teams. (p. 1)

The lawsuit seeks to create equal access to high school sports for all students, regardless of race. As the suit details, access to school sports benefits students' mental well-being, physical health, can enhance college opportunities, and can also contribute to the development of team skills such as solidarity, collaboration, and friendships, which foster community.

Final Thoughts

Upon high school graduation, Diego was awarded a scholarship to play basketball at a Division II university and he was also discriminated against by a coach. Upset with these experiences, Diego decided he did not want to endure these aggressions anymore. He left behind his passion for basketball and attended another university. Currently, he is twenty-eight years old and, more than ever, he continues to be a victim of discrimination now at his present job. As his mother, I cannot defend him the way I used to when he was a child. Obviously, Diego is now an adult and, furthermore, the discrimination he experiences nowadays is more subtle and more difficult to confirm. Nevertheless, I try to make him aware of how Latinos are being discriminated against when it comes to applying for jobs, being paid equally or especially, what is currently happening to him, not being considered when asking for a promotion. According to Crispin Ballesteros (2015), when applying for jobs, "African Americans and Latinos are less likely than Whites to receive an interview or job offer" (Crispin Ballesteros, 2015, p. 14). In addition, Crispin Ballesteros (2015) stated that Latinos do not have the opportunity of being promoted to supervisory positions or any other higher position because employers are predisposed by negative stereotypes.

Individuals who experience employment discrimination may be negatively impacted. According to Nadal et al. (2014), racism has been linked to mental health problems such as substance abuse, lower self-concept, mental distress, and depressive symptoms. When individuals perceive and experience discrimination in their personal lives, there may be detrimental impacts on their identity development and mental well-being. Additionally, Latinos may confront difficulties in securing suitable employment due to discrimination, which puts them at a greater risk for depression (Leung et al., 2014).

As a mother, I do not regret having taught Diego that hard work, perseverance, and academic preparation are the tools to achieve his dreams. It should be that way, at least, in an unprejudiced world. I am very proud of him because, despite all the injustices he has had to endure in his life, Diego continues to have a good heart and a noble soul. I believe that, as parents, we must continue to raise our voices and fight against all kinds of discrimination for our children and for humanity.

References

Bauman, K. (2017). *School enrollment of the Hispanic population: Two decades of growth.* United States Census Bureau. https://www.census.gov/newsroom/blogs/random-samplings/2017/08/school_enrollmentof.html

Crispin Ballesteros, A. (2015). *Latino professionals' views on employment discrimination towards the Latino immigrant community* (Master's thesis). https://sophia.stkate.edu/msw_papers/434

Espinoza-Herold, M. (2003). *Issues in Latino education: Race, school culture and the politics of academic success.* Allyn and Bacon.

Leung, P., LaChapelle, A., R, Scinta, A., & Olvera, N. (2014). Factors contributing to depressive symptoms among Mexican Americans and Latinos. *Social Work, 59*(1), 42–51. https://doi.org/10.1093/sw/swt047

Nadal, K. L., Griffin, K. E., Wong, Y., Hamit, S., & Rasmus, M. (2014). The impact of racial microaggressions on mental health: Counseling implications for clients of color. *Journal of Counseling & Development, 92*(1), 57–66. https://doi.org/10.1002/j.1556-6676.2014.00130.x

National Center for Education Statistics (NCES). (2019). *The condition of education: A letter from the commissioner.* https://nces.ed.gov/programs/coe/indicator_coi.asp

New York Lawyers for the Public Interest (NYLPI). (2018). *Discrimination lawsuit filed against New York City Department of Education and Public Schools Athletic League calls for equal access to school sports.* https://nylpi.org/wp-content/uploads/2018/06/PRESS-RELEASE-SIGNED-OFF.pdf

CHAPTER 13

Every Word Is True: An Autoethnography to Unravel My Story

Babak Khoshnevisan

Autoethnography is a distinctive approach that authors can use to conduct research and unlock stories that have been silenced. This method of self-inquiry holds a strong basis in the process of research through revisiting, critically reflecting, and developing our understanding of the world. This qualitative method links the personal issues with cultural frameworks (Ellis, 2004). Therefore, in this chapter, I explicate my personal story within a specific culture where the experience takes place. Precisely, I intend to scrutinize my personal experiences within a particular educational and social context. I then attempt to portray the hardships that immigrants and international students may experience by reflecting on my own story. I conclude this chapter by putting forth lessons learned with hopes to inspire other immigrants who may share experiences similar to mine. To do this, I crafted the following questions to lead me and my audience along this narrative journey:

1. How do I, as an immigrant and international student, describe my social and familial experiences outside educational settings?
2. In what ways do I, as an immigrant and international student, encounter hardships, and how do I address potential issues such as cross-cultural misunderstandings and language barriers?

In an attempt to distance my story from realist and analytical autoethnography, the discourse shared in this chapter embraces evocative autoethnography where emotions speak for themselves. I follow the work of Ellis (1997), who argues that evocative autoethnography has unintended consequences in and of itself. This chapter aims to call attention to the value of evocative autoethnography to present the story of my life as both an international student and as an immigrant in the United States.

Uncovering and unfolding joy and sorrow are unique affordances of evocative autoethnography. In this chapter, I feel poised to share an untold layer of my life. This story could go unnoticed for years and be buried with me. Instead, I choose to use this space to share my experiences with my readers. My hope is that, by revealing my untold stories, other travelers may become empowered to share their own.

© KONINKLIJKE BRILL NV, LEIDEN, 2021 | DOI: 10.1163/9789004446182_013

Who Am I?

I am a human from mother Earth looking for peace. This is who I am and I define myself in a way people cannot *other* me during our first encounter. Traditionally speaking, I am Babak. I was born after the Islamic revolution in Iran in 1982. During the first eight years of my life, I witnessed an imposed war with a neighboring country, Iraq. For the purpose of clarity, I should mention that Iran and Iraq are two different, independent nations. Iraq was ruled by Saddam Hussein before he went crazy and attacked Iran.

During my childhood, I constantly struggled with the concept of war, politics, and the like; however, learning English during those years gave me the opportunity to listen to English-speaking radio channels and analyze their messages. I listened to different radio channels on a regular basis to enhance my listening skills. Because I was so exposed to sociopolitical news and radio programs, I began to believe that politics and political issues were woven into every fabric of my life. I found myself thinking about politics and the political aspects of incidents and even world events. My experiences might be considered strange for a kid of that age. However, this reality was how I grew up as an individual. I was often exposed to the concepts of suicide, massacre, and wars. Through this exposure, I learned how presidents declare a war, how citizens lose hope, and how people say goodbye to their loved ones. Although it might be sad to dive into the dark world of adults as a kid, this was the way my thoughts were shaped and built as I was growing up. I also became interested in the different cultural aspects of news such as dance and music. Later on, when I found that my life was drenched in politics, I tried to get along with it; I decided to continue learning English and use my skills to build a better future for myself.

I went to university in Iran and became a language teacher, a translator, and an interpreter for economic sectors both nationally and internationally. I worked as an expert on international affairs in Iran's Central Chamber of Cooperatives. I had the opportunity to meet world leaders and learn from them. Later, I participated in elections in this sector and I gained two international positions by vote. After my marriage, I felt that from an economic perspective living in Iran was tough and I needed to discover more about the world. Hence, I decided to go to the United States as an international student first and then as an immigrant.

During Obama's administration, the United States put unprecedented economic sanctions on Iran, and people were economically "crippled," as Obama named it when referring to *crippling sanctions*. People employed different ways to survive in this hard time: some led a poor life, some cut extra expenses such as trips, still others could not come up with novel strategies as they had already been living on the margins due to an imposed war that preceded these sanctions. The last stratum of this category belongs to the individuals living in extreme poverty who were cornered by these sanctions. Those people had to sell their organs to survive; this was the only option they had left.

What Happened to Me and My Family?

I first came to the United States as an international student while my wife was pregnant in Iran. The hardships of living and studying in the U.S. as an Iranian were unprecedented. Thankfully, my wife joined me a few months later after the vetting process was completed and her visa was issued. At last, we were together to support each other. Once again, we could think about our challenges, create solutions, and celebrate our successes together.

Life is not always dark; every cloud has a silver lining. The crack of dawn occurred when my baby girl was born. After her birth, our whole lives drastically changed and we could finally breathe again after months of hardships. Which hardships? Ok! Maybe it is hard to explain but bear with me. I am an Iranian, therefore, I am under a travel ban and cannot leave the United States. Also, Bank of America froze my bank account due to banking sanctions on Iranians and it took me a long time to finally unfreeze it. These events coincided with Trump's Administration where patriotic emotions and racism (re)surfaced in the United States.

In the midst of all the chaos that surrounded me, I realized that ensuring my family's financial stability would become the primary obstacle I needed to tackle. Thankfully, I found a part-time job as an instructor at INTO USF (an ESL program at the University of South Florida) which allowed me to provide a stable income for our family.

How We Tackled Life's Challenges: Our Support Systems

Having a support system in a new country can hasten the learning process be it a language or any other topic. Our first support system was our family. We were thankful to have relatives in Tampa, Florida. From the moment I moved to Tampa, my aunt-in-law has been a great help. She welcomed me when I first arrived and, with her family, they provided me with all the furniture I needed when I rented my first apartment. Also, my aunt-in-law and her family gave me rides when I needed them, informed me about the American culture, and helped my wife find a good hospital to deliver our baby. Certainly, my aunt-in-law and her family have paved the way for my wife, daughter, and me.

Another support system that made my journey more enjoyable was my classmates and faculty members both at the USF and INTO USF. Among the many faculty members who helped me in my journey at USF, my committee members—Dr. Richards, Dr. Park, and Dr. Smith—facilitated the process of my immigration. Dr. Richards is a full-time professor teaching qualitative inquiry courses, Dr. Park is an associate professor teaching instructional technology (IT) courses, and Dr. Smith is an instructor and foreign language coordinator at the College of Education. These faculty members helped me raise my daughter. In addition, they also helped me with my education as mentors, editors, and co-researchers. Because of their continuous support in my personal and professional lives, I consider them my family. As such, I call one of them, Dr. Richards, mom and she calls me son. Other faculty members at INTO USF also helped me stay on the right track, maintain a steady speed in my doctoral journey, and graduate as soon as possible. One of these faculty members, Maria Mercier, always had my back and supported me to finish my education.

Another group of people who helped me start my new life in the United States was the educators at Layla's House and Champions for Children program. These two programs teach new parents how to raise a child successfully. I cannot ignore Monica and Marlin—two educators—who taught us how to take care of our baby girl. Every gift Monica and Marlin bought for me, every kind word they expressed, and every action they took significantly contributed to my family's well-being.

Support from family, colleagues, and friends was key for me as an immigrant. For this reason, I believe that support systems are essential to increase the success of immigrant families' transition. At the same time, it is important to highlight that the support provided by my family, friends, and colleagues was not the only source of support that I received. My wife and the unity of our household was another vital support system that improved my path of immigration. My wife, Elaheh, was the most prominent part of my success in earning a Ph.D. and coping with all types of issues during our transition and settlement. She was the one who gave me the strength to fight this uphill battle of the immigration process. Equally important, my in-laws supported me whenever I needed them. My mother-in-law, Monir, did a phenomenal job in helping my wife and me whenever we felt depressed. This family support system was the light that ushered a pathway in the darkness. Without a doubt, my family paved my way to becoming the person I am today.

Lessons Learned

After reflecting on my own experiences, I have come to realize that support systems are essential to increase the success of immigrant families' transition. I have learned that, at times of crisis, including immigration, support systems are essential for people. I have also learned that making new friends and participating in new environments was necessary for my success in this new country.

In my experience, the sooner an immigrant becomes familiar with the host country's culture, the better. The accompanying stress and anxiety can be obviated if people from the host culture can be your entourage. I learned to make friends. I learned to be an observer. I learned to explore and witness the unknown. The more I interacted with people outside of my circle and comfort zone, the sooner my fears melted into love, harmony, and kindness. My family and I made a concerted effort to participate in as many cultural festivals as possible. We participated in cultural and religious ceremonies of different people who came from all around the world. Living in the United States has been an opportunity to explore the similarities between my own culture and other cultures. At the same time, exposure to diverse cultures has allowed me to make human connections and overcome barriers. I have learned that barriers can restrict our growth as individuals. For this reason, my family and I try to challenge preconceived notions and turn the unknown into new opportunities to learn and accept. Through this journey, I have found that tolerance is the key. I now practice tolerance toward people, cultures, and religions that differ from the ones I am accustomed to. For me, being an immigrant has been, and will continue to be, a life-long learning quest.

Final Thoughts

Immigration is a topic that notoriously imposes new challenges in the life of immigrants. As an immigrant, I encountered numerous difficulties that extend well beyond the events shared in this chapter. However, I share my story hoping readers will be able to reflect and learn from my experiences. What I learned in my immigration process is that newcomers need to establish support systems, stay open to new cultures and cultural events, and seek success stories to learn from other immigrants. Practicing these three lessons can open up new avenues in the process of immigration. As I end this piece, I hope my story can guide other immigrants and provide them with ways through which they can facilitate and scaffold their immigration process.

References

Ellis, C. (1997). Evocative autoethnography: Writing emotionally about our lives. In W. G. Tierney & Y. S. Lincoln (Eds.), *Representation and the text: Re-framing the narrative voice* (pp. 115–139). State University of New York Press.

Ellis, C. (2004). *The ethnographic I: A methodological novel about autoethnography*. Alta Mira Press.

CHAPTER 14

Quê Hương

Ethan Tính Trịnh

I have not recovered yet from an illness, I thus took a week off from work to recover. I am sitting alone in a small apartment when a chilly breeze reminds me that fall is here in Georgia, United States (U.S.). Whenever I stop working, I am alone. Whenever I am alone, I think about Vietnam. Even though my physical body is in Georgia, my mind always travels back to Vietnam. Every time I miss *quê hương*, I whisper the poem/song "*Quê hương*" written by Vietnamese poet Đỗ Trung Quân. The melancholy, the loneliness, and the fatigue control my body and make it difficult for my fingers to type on the keyboard. The fabrics of liminal space in this apartment, in this country, freeze my soul and body. I cannot move anywhere else beyond this space. However, listening to *Quê hương* (Nguyen, 2010) heals the dryness of my soul, watering it for recovery.

Quê hương mỗi người chỉ một	*Quê hương* everyone has only one
Như là chỉ một Mẹ thôi	It's like you only have one mother
Quê hương nếu ai không nhớ	*Quê hương,* if you don't remember
Sẽ không lớn nổi thành người	You won't grow up as a human being

My translation for this poem/song is raw, rocky, and unsmooth. I admit my weakness in translating Vietnamese into English. I spent time finding a "good" translation for each word; I spent time thinking whether my translation successfully described what the author truly meant; I hesitated in this translation, in my *own* language. I think I failed in this translation. I did not want to give an English version at first, but the readers, specifically Vietnamese-Americans, will appreciate this raw attempt because it could help them trace lost identities of language and history. In addition, translating is a political act; it is not just linguistic translation; instead, it is an expansion of a soul, memories, culture, and politics into each word. Translating is not a skill, it is a wholeness of identities of one's life. Therefore, for the rest of this essay, I will not italicize the word quê hương or any Vietnamese words because this is my claim as an act of resistance against the western academic writing style I am trained to publish in.

Quê hương means "country" or "homeland" in English, but the English translation sets physical, linguistic, and emotional boundaries for immigrants like us. For Vietnamese people, these English translations do not fully embrace or describe the authenticity, complexity, and richness of the word itself as our quê hương transcends physical spaces or boundaries. Likewise, it is hard and burdensome to describe my nỗi nhớ quê hương (or missing one's country). This phrase sounds as complex as it means. It is complex in a way that I write about my country in a host country. It is complex in a way that I do not know if I still belong to my home country when I am now holding a different identity in my driver's license. It is complex in a way that I stand in-between spaces of political borders between two countries (i.e. the U.S. and Vietnam). I thus get lost in my nỗi nhớ quê hương. I thus get lost in an act of translation. In fact, it has been five years since I stopped reading Vietnamese literature; I feel I am not competent at neither writing nor explaining in my home language. But one thing for sure is that I miss my quê hương now.

This nỗi nhớ quê hương (missing one's country) is different from the nỗi nhớ my mom used to feel when she was waiting for my dad at the cemetery while he was away from Vietnam after the 1986's Vietnamese Economic Reform. In 2018, as I wrote my autoethnography, *How hugging mom teaches me the meaning of love and perhaps beyond*, I spoke from my heart and critical mind to give agency to Vietnamese moms and other women of color who suffer from domestic violence and abuse. In that autoethnographic piece, I wrote to challenge societal patriarchy, which causes open, unhealed, intergenerational wounds. In addition, I described the different phases of nỗi nhớ in different contexts. However, in the chapter of this book, I use the term nỗi nhớ to express emotions, feelings, and oftentimes hopelessness, experienced by the children who have to travel far away from their homelands, as well as by those who are unable to come back to their homelands for political and financial reasons. Further, I prefer to not theorize in this piece. This sounds academic and distant to Vietnamese peoples and non-academic readers if they suddenly run into this space. The more theory and academic words I use, the more I push and distance myself and my peoples far away from our quê hương. I thus want to stay true to my feelings, my soul, my stories, my translation. Finally, before discovering what quê hương looks like, I ask you to *co*-imagine with me, so we can return to our quê hương at the end of this piece.

Quê Hương Is out of Reach

Since I immigrated to the United States (U.S.), often called the land of opportunities, in 2015, I have experienced a mixture of feelings. The complexity of emotions, feelings, misery, insecurity, oppositionality, insider-outsider binary has been weaving, squeezing my heart and my mind, bringing me to moments of silence where I just sit still and face vulnerabilities—by myself. I acknowledge I was privileged to know English when I arrived here; I also acknowledge my privilege of having a shelter to stay during the first few months after arrival and being able to afford a car to drive to work. However, I acknowledge that I had no quê hương to go back to. My parents sold our small house in Vietnam before we headed to the United States. Probably, when we decided to leave Vietnam, we decided to cut off our physical and emotional attachments to quê hương. The unknown and unspoken meaning of "the land of opportunities" held the utmost power, which pushed us to eradicate our identities, our attachment to come back to quê hương. On the day we stepped onto the plane to the U.S. in December 2015, our tears were left behind, hugs were left behind, attachments were left behind—on the soil of Vietnam. We committed to leaving. Our quê hương is now too far, far away in space and time—out of reach—to go back.

I think I need to take a break to b r e a t h e...

The melancholy, the loneliness, and the fatigue overwhelmingly control my body and it is making it difficult for my fingers to type on the keyboard.

Quê Hương Is Fragments of Cultural Values

I am whispering, following with its melodic song "Quê hương." This song is such a beautiful lullaby that lures me to sleep, to fly back to a childhood memory—a rice field where farmers were harvesting the fully ripe grains. This song also flies me to wooden cottages where we, Vietnamese kids, were flying colorful paper kites in the sky, the sky of freedom, of childhood, of ice creams. In this memory, we were also playing a năm mười game where one person closes their eyes, then the rest of us find a place to hide. We were laughing out loud, chasing each other until all of us were exhausted. Then we were lying on the hay, smelling the dryness of the grass and the smoke coming from the grass being burned by the farmers at the end of a working day. My friends and I were giggling, looking at the blue sky, telling each other what we wanted to do when we grew up. Then we were given mía by the local farmers. Mía is a Mekong Delta's tropical stem with its green skin outside, but the sweetness could quench our thirst after playing games. Mía soon became an exquisite drink that we, the village children, would often crave. Lying down, having mía, we were singing bắc kim thang, a folk song in the South of Vietnam, which tells a story we did not fully understand, but we learned the lyrics by heart since we were little. The memories from the song, the heat in the field, the laughter during and after the game have been always there, staying in a special place within me, my parents, and other Vietnamese immigrants who left the country for whatever reason. These memories will probably stay with us until our last breath. Further, the memories will be shared with our future generations so that they can know a bit about their parents and their ancestors in Vietnam.

The song "Quê hương" is still playing, my childhood's memories are being retrieved and are coming alive; they are flying me to a dreamy land in Mekong Delta, Vietnam. Mekong Delta is beautiful in a way that only children from this region can understand and appreciate. Mekong Delta, in my memories, was peaceful; there were no skyscrapers, there were no luxury cars. It was, and still is, beautiful in its own way.

I miserably love and miss the feeling of when I was a kid, sitting on a small-sized, tightly-woven, bamboo boat, which my grandma called xuồng. My grandma was a great paddler; she was skillful at propelling xuồng, steering it beautifully so that I could place my tiny hands into the cold water and play with it. My grandma always sang "Quê hương" while she was paddling; the sound, the scene, the voice, all of which intertwined and has become an important piece in my heart then and now.

Quê hương là con diều biếc	Quê hương is a kite
Tuổi thơ con thả trên đồng	Your childhood is a kite, you fly it in the field
Quê hương là con đò nhỏ	Quê hương is a small boat
Êm đềm khua nước ven sông	Quietly moving but echoing in a river

Quê hương is fragments of cultural values, of pieces of childhood memories, sounds, voices, images, places that we—Vietnamese immigrants, Vietnamese-Americans, and other immigrants—preciously call "home." Even though we live in a distant space where we are far away from our homelands, even though we are being isolated and disconnected from our own home language, even though we cannot sit on a boat to play with the cold water or fly a kite in the field, our memories about our homelands, our quê hương are not eradicated, regardless of the power of the country that we are residing, i.e. The United States of America.

Quê Hương Is a Lost Dream

I am writing, continuing to listen to the song. Suddenly, I hear the sound of an airplane in the sky. The sound reminds me of the flight our family had taken in 2015; the flight that (dis)connected us between two worlds: the U.S. and

Vietnam. It was such a long 24-hour flight; the flight that brought me to the world that everyone in Vietnam has dreamt of but, at the same time, the flight that took me away from my homeland, my country, my quê hương. Before taking off, I got a tattoo with the date we left our country; the same day our family stepped on a Korean airline and left quê hương behind, even though I already had my dream job. I had been teaching English as a Second Language for five years in Vietnam, but my dad insisted, "Đi đi, qua Mỹ sẽ có tương lai hơn!" (Go, go to America, it will be a better future!). Similar to the pronoun *it* in his sentence, which is unknown and unclear, our future remained the same.

We, as a family, could not define how better the future would be, except for the fact that we all came to this country with a suitcase of hope, of a better future, and a *"work hard and you will achieve anything"* ideology. None of us in the family at that time knew what would await us; we were strangers in this land of opportunities; the land where people would sacrifice anything to come to, even their lives. Our family had been waiting for thirteen years to get a visa to this country. "What is the difference between quê hương here and there?" I myself wondered that before we came to the United States. However, no one has ever asked me if I had Vietnamese dreams. I understand American dreams are powerful, unspoken statements, ideologies, and the reasons why immigrants come for. Nonetheless, we immigrants still have our dreams, too, but ours seem to be silenced and unvoiced in the power of a dominant country where new immigrants struggle to navigate and (re)settle. In the moments of struggles and negotiations in terms of languages and identities, whether staying or leaving, we find different ways to survive and thrive.

Quê Hương Is a Rebellion to Assimilations

Assimilation is a process in which a person who comes to a host country has to give up their own identities in terms of language, culture, original names, and accents. The power of assimilation is huge, irresistible, dangerous, and toxic to each immigrant, whether you agree with me or not. I used to lose myself in the assimilation process.

When I first came to the U.S., the first thing I did was to reject my language. In other words, I chose to only speak the language of this country, American English, so that English speakers would not discriminate against me because of where I came from. I spoke English with pride so that I could hide my identities. I spoke English to assimilate into this country. I wrote and thought about everything in English. I put all my Vietnamese books away, inside a suitcase, to train myself to think and speak "as an American." The suitcase that

I brought from Vietnam, which contained Vietnamese books, dreams, hopes, was replaced with (self) hatred and shame.

I lost myself to the assimilation process—quickly and completely.

• • •

But, after a long process of unpacking my identities, I am now learning how to unlearn the assimilation process. By reclaiming my uniqueness, my immigration status, my languages, my accentedness, I am proud of who I am. One of the things I am doing to unlearn assimilation behaviors is to bring my culture into my scholarly work. As you can see, I am attempting to bring Vietnamese music in this piece; I want to add this beautiful cultural piece into academic western literature as well. In a piece I wrote about hugging my mom and how her eternal love teaches me social justice and equality, the very first piece of myself that was published in a western archive, I found the courage to use bài hát ru con, a Vietnamese folk song, as a starting point of my story. This time, I am finding that courage again, holding my breath, attempting to weave "Quê hương" into this space. I feel comfortable, safe, and home-y since parts of my identities will be appreciated here. I am feeling this space will accept and welcome me back to my quê hương, my homeland, my language, my Vietnamese-ness, and Asian-ness. I am feeling that I am coming back to Vietnam; I am sitting on xuồng where my grandma is steering on the water. I am coming back home in this space, and I hope you are coming home, too.

Another reason I attempt to add Vietnamese dân ca (or folk songs) into the western literature is because I truly want to build a bridge to connect with hyphenated Vietnamese people who are living inside and outside of the U.S., or for those who are living a life between two separate countries, like me. Writing this piece creates a space for people like us to come back to our cultures and appreciate our language and memories. I, therefore, urge you to consider bringing beautiful, unique cultural values into your future pieces of writing. I, therefore, urge you to feel proud of your mother tongues, your heritage, your homeland, your quê hương's language because they are invaluable assets in each of us—regardless of whether you have successfully passed the naturalization test in your host country, changed your name, and/or put a hyphen in the middle of your nationality, Vietnamese-American for instance.

There are words that I want to keep in Vietnamese ways; I refuse to translate them into English. Because if I do, I am afraid, I could not express what quê hương truly is. Because if I do, I would lose my identity, my language, my memories again. This time, if I do, I would lose them forever. I would forever give up my soul and mind to the language of the colonizers. I refuse to do so. I am still a Vietnamese child who was born and grew up in Vietnam. I am, thus, my quê hương. I am, thus, my language.

Quê Hương Is Relational

Even though there are different interpretations of what quê hương looks like and how is viewed, I have my own connections with this simple phrase. I prefer not to bring demographic statistics in this essay because I am not good at using statistics to tell a story; I am not a quantitative person. However, throughout this chapter, we have *co*-imagined what my quê hương looks like. Our five senses were awakened to taste the sweetness of sugar cane (mía), to hear the laughter of the kids, to smell the liveliness of grass hay, to touch the cold, fresh water in the river, and to visualize the simplicity and beautifulness of parts of my quê hương. I thus hope I could unfold parts of your quê hương by sharing mine. I truly hope that I removed the rigidity and stricture of academics to liberate us from the liminal, physical space of this country and fly us to our own quê hương. Quê hương is no longer a personal sentiment, but quê hương is now relational to all of us who shared parts of our identities, our nỗi nhớ quê hương together.

As we have come this far together, I am curious, "What does quê hương look like in you, who are far away from your quê hương?" You do not have to answer right now, but we will find another space for this question. Now, I need to rest my eyes, my mind, my fingers, and turn on the song "Quê Hương," or simply just take a meditation walk (Trinh, 2020) so I can get some physical, emotional, and spiritual recovery.

References

Nguyen, T. (2010, December 13). Quê Hương Là Chùm Khế Ngọt [Video file]. https://www.youtube.com/watch?v=bFii5TFgdpM

Trinh, E. (2018). How hugging mom teaches me the meaning of love and perhaps beyond. *The Journal of Faith, Education, and Community, 2*(1), 1–14.

Trinh, E. (2020). "Still you resist": An autohistoria-teoria of a Vietnamese queer teacher to meditate, teach, and love in the Coatlicue State. *International Journal of Qualitative Studies in Education, 33*(6), 621–633. https://doi.org/10.1080/09518398.2020.1747662

CHAPTER 15

I Lost My Language But Your Child Doesn't Have To

May F. Chung

Becoming Cantonese

Gloria E. Anzaldúa (1987) once wrote about people stuck in a sense of linguistic and cultural loss, "As a people who have been stripped of our history, language, identity, and pride, we attempt again and again to find what we have lost digging into our cultural roots imaginatively and making art out of our findings" (p. 176). My own exploration into bilingual identity was thus also impacted by my cultural upbringing.

My first language is Cantonese, which is the language of my culture, my customs, my heritage, and the food that I love. Every time I would get angry or frustrated, I would immediately resort to phrases of insult in Cantonese. It was the language I would use to fight with my siblings as we were growing up. When we would close down our family restaurant and eat poached chicken with ginger scallion oil on Chinese New Year, I would pray to my ancestors in Chinese.[1] All of my parents' habits would be given in a voice that was astute, multi-toned, lively, and ambitious. This *was* my mother tongue.

I grew up in a small town of North Carolina, in the foothills of the Appalachian Mountains, in a town with a receding manufacturing industry. Growing up, my family was the only Chinese family in the area. Therefore, as I enrolled in school, it became clear that no one spoke my mother tongue. Immediately, I was put in an English as a second language (ESL) class with individualized lessons. English became a hard language to grapple with, so far removed from the warm embrace of the sounds I was raised in. I remember feeling lost, constantly searching for someone to understand me, for someone I could understand. This feeling always stayed with me, and it is one of the reasons why I pursued linguistics as an area of interest and teach ESL.

Losing Chinese for English

As I began to grasp more English, I began to lose parts of my native Chinese. When classmates at school would ask me to pronounce certain words, I would refuse to speak Chinese because I was ashamed and resented the fact that

© KONINKLIJKE BRILL NV, LEIDEN, 2021 | DOI: 10.1163/9789004446182_015

my parents always spoke English with an accent. Instead, I tried to find ways in which I could become more "American," favoring fast food and American music over my parents' traditional cooking and popular Cantopop.

What made matters worse was that I began to see my Chinese decline. I stopped responding back in Chinese to my parents and, gradually, spoke more and more in English. My parents became increasingly frustrated about my lack of Chinese. "*Ai ya!*"[2] my dad would exclaim, "*jook-sing m sik gong Gwóngdūng wá*" (The bamboo pole[3] doesn't speak Cantonese). And I often reflected on just how right he was, "Why *can't* I speak Chinese?" After a while, my parents begrudgingly accommodated my responses in English, but often critiqued how they struggled to communicate Chinese concepts in another language, especially one so foreign to them. To this date, my parents and I continue our conversations in English, never managing to get over the linguistic wall between us.

When Bilingualism Subtracts

Unfortunately, my story sounds all too familiar to many Americans. I am one of many children of immigrants who cannot speak their native language well or at all, especially in the United States, where the expectation to learn English leads to the loss of many heritage languages. This type of phenomenon, known as "subtractive bilingualism," is what Wong-Fillmore (1991) discusses as a plight of "countless American immigrant and native children and adults who have lost their ethnic languages in the process of becoming linguistically assimilated into the English-speaking world of the school and society" (p. 324).

In particular, speakers of Asian languages are especially in danger of losing their native tongues possibly due to the lack of access to those languages in the community and society at large. Another factor could be the dominance of English, especially its status as the language needed for academic success and upward mobility in the United States. As Shin (2005) mentions, immigrant parents often fear that their children will "not learn English quickly enough and thus fall behind in school" (p. 7). This fear and pressure of children trailing behind in academics manifest in parents wanting to speak English to children at home, instead of the native language. As a result, many children of immigrants grow up speaking primarily English, while losing proficiency in their native tongues.

While I reflect upon my own language experiences and become disappointed by my lack of language skills in Chinese, I am also curious about why some parents want to retain the native language, despite societal pressures.

What draws me to investigating the experiences of parental motivations is wondering, "Why do some parents want to teach their children the heritage language while others do not?" This question has stayed with me and has motivated me through my own career trajectory.

Uncovering the Bilingual Possibilities

The turning point for my interest in bilingualism came when, as part of my teaching practicum, my professor recommended that I observe a dual language school in Chapel Hill, North Carolina. This was a new kind of instruction model, one that offered bilingual education in Mandarin Chinese and English, with the classroom consisting of speakers of both languages. At first glance, it was a surprise to see both children who looked like me and children of all different ethnicities and racial backgrounds speaking together in Mandarin. I asked the teacher whether the school was primarily for Chinese or English-speaking backgrounds, and she responded "both." For English-speaking students, it opens doors to another world of culture and new ways of thinking. "What about for Chinese students?" I asked.

The teacher then pointed to a Chinese student in her class, a small girl with two braided pigtails. "She just arrived in the U.S. a week ago," she said. For me, it was mind-boggling to know that she, like me, was a student who spoke a language different from her peers but unlike me, her peers could speak it back. For Chinese students, they got to feel like they belonged in an American classroom. In watching the girl interact with her peers, she did not seem to carry the same shame I had in harboring a secret language no one could understand. Instead, she seemed like any other child, laughing and playing along with the other children in her grade. It was an eye-opener to see my culture featured in my home state, on the main stage, as something someone wanted to learn. For once, being Chinese was something that was valued. My culture and heritage were on display as something *good*. The little girl and all the children I saw in the classroom that day will have so many more opportunities than I ever had. That moment changed my life.

One Moment Becomes a Mission

From that instant, I wanted to become a champion for bilingual education. When I graduated with my ESL licensure and got my first job teaching in an elementary school, I became not only an educator but also an advocate for my students and their native languages. There were times when I would step in to intervene on a student's behalf, or actively work with the teachers to allow opportunities for their students to share their cultural and linguistic backgrounds. From the beginning, the teachers were hesitant and would ask me to translate for their ESL kids for something as simple as bringing in their lunch money, but over the years, I would work with my fellow educators so they felt comfortable enough to communicate with their English learners.

As teachers, sometimes we set the tone for our classroom cultures, whether we intend to or not. Classrooms can be intimidating, isolated institutions that demand much of young children to "perform" in a language they are learning. On the other hand, teachers can make their classroom into a refuge, where they can experiment in English and also be surrounded by the comfort of their language of nurture. A teacher can make their students feel included by just being interested in their background and believe that what they have to say is important.

For older students, or for those like me, who have lost or who have started to lose their native languages, teachers can help bridge that connection between home and school by connecting some of the links. For example, I encouraged the parents of my ESL students to speak in their native languages at home and also invited parents to write a letter in their home language addressed to their child. In class, I invited my students to decipher their personal letter using dictionaries and tools like Google Translate. In class, their children could not only strengthen their linguistic skills but also remain proud of their own cultures and languages.

Often, teachers confide to me that they want to support their children's languages, but they are not sure how to start. The teachers, themselves, may be monolingual and do not have the language skills or resources to get started. My advice is always to start small. Teachers—monolingual or not—can be helpful by giving their students the gift of time. In the pressures of standardized testing, sometimes the most helpful gift is the gift of time. Learn to be patient with learners as they navigate a new language. Give children, especially young children, the time to explore their second language at their own pace.

The important thing to know is that there are many resources, support, and funds of knowledge that teachers can tap into. Community members are often a source that many teachers can reach out to become classroom readers and helpers. They can also become pivotal key figures to lend language support for English language learners. Community members also serve an important role in cultural transmission, and can read books, tell stories, play instruments, or sing songs in their native language. Teachers can invite community members in the classroom so students have a comfortable language to retreat to but also have someone who motivates them to try their second language.

Today I am an ESL teacher so I can be that voice for parents that tells them to embrace their native tongues. I want to tell them my story that, by teaching English every day, I do so with pain to reconcile my own native language and culture. Advocating for bilingual education offers me a chance to promote Chinese, a language and culture I was once ashamed of and resented, to become appreciated and even coveted in an institutionalized setting of a school. I may have lost my voice, my Chinese voice, but at the cost of knowledge and a resolved mission to ensure that young people, just like the girl I saw in the classroom that day, can remain confident in their bilingual identities.

The Prodigal Daughter Returns

As for my siblings and I, even though we primarily communicate in English, we find ourselves inserting Cantonese when there is not a translation that fits or when we want to speak privately about someone without them knowing. Now when I am speaking with my own parents, my ears are more interested in their words, and sometimes I will repeat back their phrases. They may think I am listening intently, but actually I am re-learning the language!

Last year, I was en route to visit a friend in Macau and had an opportunity for a quick stopover in Hong Kong. Almost instantly, I felt my Cantonese returning. I was able to recognize certain words here or there and recognize the tones. As I began to voice the sounds myself, I found my mother tongue coming back—and I realized that it never truly went away. My native language was like a box that I put away on a shelf in the back of a closet. Over the years, it has gathered dust, but I find that I can return to unpack that box—and still return to the familiar sights and sounds.

I remember stopping in a cafe where an elderly waitress asked me a question.

"*Sek teng mm sek gong* (I can understand, but I can't speak)" I responded in Cantonese. She smiled and responded that her own granddaughter who lived in Canada was just like me. There were many overseas Chinese who grew up in Western countries and did not learn their native language, she remarked. But it did not make them any less Chinese.

"*Jook-sing*," I asked?

"*Jook-sing*," she winked.

I may be a bamboo pole, but as it turns out: I am still a bamboo.

Notes

1   Chinese can consist of many different dialects. More famously, it is used interchangeably with Mandarin, a language spoken by 800 million people (or about 70% of Chinese nationals). However, the Chinese of my heritage language is Cantonese, spoken by 68 million, and prominently used by speakers from Hong Kong, Macau, and Guangdong province. For this essay, unless noted otherwise, I use Chinese to refer to my native language, Cantonese, as a sense of reclamation and a recognition that we are Chinese, too.

2   Every child growing up in a Cantonese household is familiar with this popular exclamation, similar to "Oh my God!" in English, but with a mixture of anger, exasperation, and disappointment.

3   "Jook-sing," which means "bamboo pole" or "bamboo rod" in Cantonese is often a derogatory term for Chinese Americans and other overseas Chinese who are perceived to identify more with Western culture and beliefs than with that of their Asian heritage. The bamboo represents an Asian countenance, while being hollow on the inside.

References

Anzaldúa, G. (1987). *Borderlands/La frontera: The new mestiza.* Aunt Lute Books.

Shin, S. J. (2005). *Developing in two languages: Korean children in America.* Multilingual Matters Ltd.

Wong-Fillmore, L. (1991). When learning a second language means losing the first. *Early Childhood Research Quarterly, 6*(3), 323–346. https://doi.org/10.1016/S0885-2006(05)80059-6

CHAPTER 16

Pagbabalik: Does It Even Matter?

Sandy Tadeo

The French novelist André Gide (1973) wrote, "One doesn't discover new lands without consenting to lose sight, for a very long time, of the shore" (p. 353). Throughout the years, this quote has remained with me because it represents my past life. At the same time, this quote resonates with me today more than ever as I find the courage to explore uncharted paths into my future. In this chapter, I share my story of struggle and (pending) transformation.

Dreaming

A Philippine Airline flight departed from the airport in Manila over two decades ago and landed at the Honolulu airport in Hawai'i. That warm September day in 1999 changed everything for my family and me as we began our journey into our new adopted country. My parents hauled their luggage and their *balik-bayan*[1] boxes along with their four children to temporarily stay at our cousins' house on the island of Maui, Hawai'i. There, in that small dwelling, we resided temporarily in one of the cramped bedrooms where six of my family members had to share a space. However, this difficulty did not discourage us. My family and I recognized it as a small part of the bigger picture because it was the very beginning of our American dreams.

The first few days in Hawai'i felt as if we were truly living in paradise. We had heard of the wonders of Hawai'i and the United States in general, but actually living in it was an entirely different experience. My uncle, aunt, and cousins provided us with our earliest memories that, until this day, remain truly unforgettable. In those early days, they drove us around the magnificent island, took us trekking to a breathtaking dormant volcano, brought us to enormous big-box stores and grocery stores with their shelves brimming with stock, drove us through a nice fast-food restaurant to pick up lunch, and most importantly they took us to see our new schools. These memories, as joyous as they might seem, often return to me with accompanying sadness. Back then, my siblings and I were excited to explore these new experiences but now as an adult, I understand the sacrifices my cousins were making to welcome us into the

© KONINKLIJKE BRILL NV, LEIDEN, 2021 | DOI: 10.1163/9789004446182_016

United States. They had taken their time to receive us and introduce us to their way of life but with a price. They had taken time off from their busy schedules and spent their hard-earned money on us so that we could have these unforgettable experiences.

After enjoying Hawai'i for about a week, it quickly became apparent that being multilingual was a necessity. To be able to speak three different languages or being multilingual in, namely Ilocano, Tagalog, and English, at the age of fourteen enabled me to simultaneously communicate with my grandparents and old friends in the Philippines, as well as relatives and newly-found friends, classmates, neighbors, and acquaintances in Hawai'i. In that short amount of time when we were introduced to the island, I could hear the amalgamation of words in many different languages being spoken all around me. If I could describe that experience in a metaphor, I would say that it was like listening to incoherent music that was difficult to understand but you concentrate on its tune and become enthralled with its melody. These are my earliest memories of living in the United States and I am forever grateful for having them.

Ascending

As we began our journey into the United States school system, we had to learn how to adjust at a very quick pace. My oldest sister had been studying to become a nurse in the Philippines but had to stop her studies in order to immigrate to the United States. Once we were settled in Hawai'i, she decided to look into continuing her nursing degree at the community college. But soon enough, she was quickly discouraged by the culture shock that she had experienced. As a result, she disregarded her studies altogether.

On the other hand, my two younger sisters and I were thrown into the American school system after only a couple of weeks of being in Hawai'i. My sisters and I quickly learned that everyone was on their own, in finding their niche, their cliques, and fitting into where they belonged. Faces of different colors and shapes greeted us or rather, ignored us while we boarded the school bus on our way to register for classes, in which we were already a few weeks behind. That was the very first time that we rode on a school bus; it was only possible for us to see a yellow school bus on television before that moment. The idea of forming a line to get into a bus (or for anything, for that matter) was also a new concept for us. We were not used to those habits which were part of the American culture. Nonetheless, we were given a few disapproving looks and scowls as we found our way on the back of the line.

On a short ascend to the hilltop by the school bus, we listened intently and very nervously as tongues of different sounds and foreign words reverberated throughout the bus. As I stepped out of the bus, I became overwhelmed instantaneously as a large number of people emerged into view; coming out of cars, spilling out of soccer-mom vans and other school buses. It was like when you accidentally looked straight at the sun and realized that you had to close your eyes or you would become blinded by it. I became frightened and disoriented as I found my way to the registrar's office. I could barely speak English so it was difficult for me to communicate with anyone. Trying to find a Filipino student in an American high school who could speak Tagalog or Ilocano and who was also friendly to a newcomer like me was like finding a needle in a haystack.

Searching

As soon as I started school in the ninth grade here in the United States, I was compelled to discover my individuality. Interestingly enough, knowing that I was timid and introverted, I also wanted to stand out. I wanted to exceed in all that I undertook and be distinctive from my classmates. Although I was multilingual, I understood that my beginner proficiency in English was more powerful than my fluency in the other two languages (Tagalog and Ilocano). I wanted to find a way to not only improve my skills in English but to become better than my peers. I was competitive in that way.

Incidentally, I realized I was also improving my speaking and writing skills in my second language, Tagalog, as time went on living in Hawai'i. Being immersed in an environment where many different languages were spoken all at the same time was both fascinating and reinforcing. Many of my newly-found friends spoke a combination of Tagalog and Ilocano, or other Philippine languages. The only way for us, Filipino immigrants, to communicate would be to speak the national language of the Philippines (officially standardized as Filipino, but commonly known as Tagalog) and that was how I was able to improve my language skills.

Accommodating

One person who was a tremendous help in my school work, and also in my personal life, was my math teacher Ms. Akey. I first met Ms. Akey when I demanded to be transferred from Pre-Algebra to regular Algebra because I was not being

stimulated in the former class. She was instrumental in making a huge difference in my life as a student and as a newly-arrived immigrant in the United
States. Ms. Akey would stay back every day after school to tutor anyone who
was willing to stay behind to complete their homework with her. As time went
on, I discovered that I was not only learning math but also English. Being in her
after-school tutoring sessions improved my problem-solving skills, as well as
my computer and English communication skills. Ms. Akey was my teacher for
three out of four years in high school maths and I was in her tutoring sessions
almost on a daily basis. She was my biggest influence and I owe her a great deal
on learning analytical and reasoning skills, computer skills, communications
skills, as well as people skills.

Realizing

As part of our career preparation programs, we had a guest speaker in one
of my high school classes. She was a commercial airline pilot and she must
have been very happy in her chosen profession because she spoke very pas-
sionately about it. I do not remember much of what she said, except for one
thing. She mentioned that knowing more than one language would be a
very valuable asset and that we should focus on learning *helpful* languages
such as Japanese, Mandarin, or Spanish and to forget about the "dead languages," such as Tagalog, Vietnamese, or other less popular languages. For a
while, I felt upset and confused that an important person in our community
would say such a thing about my languages, but I would soon learn of its
true meaning.

   The pilot meant that learning other languages would transport me to better places and bring in more opportunities in the future. For me, however, her
words meant that learning and improving my English skills would provide me
with better possibilities later in life. I would be able to not only go to college
but to get accepted in prestigious universities. I would be able to expand my
career choices and not have to struggle working for the tourism industry,
which makes up a large portion of Hawai'i's economy. I witnessed how my
family and friends working at resorts had to often maintain multiple jobs to
make ends meet and I wanted, in the words of André Gide, to discover new
oceans so I found the courage to lose sight of the Maui shores. As I grew older,
I started to realize that in our society, especially in the American system of
consumerism, language is a currency. I became aware that knowing the English
language would make new social spaces available to me and would also lead
me to better opportunities.

Serving

At the age of 17, I abruptly asked my parents to sign an age waiver for me so that I could join the U.S. Marine Corps. They were both dumbfounded as they witnessed the recruiter, who was dressed in a military dress uniform, walk up the stairs to get to our second-floor apartment where my mother was cooking dinner. My parents signed that waiver and I left for boot camp three months after I graduated high school. I left behind my college admissions, the potential to have been a part of the tourism industry in Hawai'i, and my beloved family to pursue a treacherous path and a mysterious future.

Joining the U.S. military was both an impulsive and important decision for me. Signing the military contract and completing the training would be a major step in getting closer to having a better life. The Veterans Affairs' (VA) GI Bill program would eventually pay for my associate's, bachelor's, and master's degrees.

Improving

Surprisingly, as I became farther and farther away from home, I also started to improve my broken English. At the same time, I learned that having wit and a sense of humor were important survival skills while serving in the military. I had to both learn how to have a sense of humor and understand the jokes that were being said, all in English. To learn military commands would also prove to be difficult while still learning English. Compounded by hearing the words with many different accents, it threw a wrench into the works. Additionally, getting to figure out the many different American idiomatic expressions just threw me out of the loop. In all my endeavors, I always tried to find improvements for myself. To become proficient in English, I set my mind to speaking full sentences, giving feedback on conversations, and even partake in arguments.

"Hablo"[2]

After completing my first four years of honorable military service, I decided to reenlist in the U.S. Marine Corps for a second time. Luckily, I was sent to serve in Quito, Ecuador as my first duty station at the U.S. Embassy there. South Americans were adamant about speaking only in Spanish and refused to learn even an ounce of English. This forced me to learn and start speaking Spanish.

As it was with English, I believed that learning Spanish was advantageous for me in improving my chances of having a better career. I acquired conversational skills in Spanish for the duration of my stay in Ecuador, which was an entire year. I was able to communicate with the local employees and citizens of that country and partake in their conversations. I was able to explore Quito and its surrounding places with little help from my Spanish instructor and colleagues. In addition, I was able to perform business deals, as part of my military duties, in the local language with successful outcomes. After completing my obligations in Ecuador, I also lived in France and Nepal. I, however, was not as successful in learning French and Nepali as I did with Spanish.

Studying

I left the U.S. Marine Corps after completing eight years of honorable service. As I attempted to trudge along in the "civilian world" (as they call it in the military), the path of least resistance led me to a decision to continue going to college. The Veteran Affairs paid for me to complete my bachelor's degree and also my master's degree after leaving the military. I am indebted to my spouse, who is an educator and life-long learner, in encouraging me and supporting me throughout this process. He encouraged me to pursue a master's degree to better improve my chances in getting jobs as well as to continue my learning even further. Quite honestly, I was motivated in pursuing a graduate degree after seeing that my husband had completed three of his own, and then pursued a Ph.D.

Becoming

After living in this country for so long, I recognize that being proficient in English has more weight than being fluent in my first two languages. It has taken me time and much reflection to accept this fact, but Ilocano and Tagalog cannot ensure me or my family economic stability in the United States. As I witness my declining proficiency in my native and second languages, I continue to experience the rewards attached to the marketability that English provides. Quickly, English has become my primary language on my daily interactions at work, with my spouse at home, and with my family when we talk over the phone. Many times, I catch myself struggling to remember words and phrases in Ilocano and Tagalog; these events become more common as days go by. Losing my languages has slowly become one of the most regretful circumstances of my life; to succeed in the U.S., I must continue to improve my English to be afforded more professional opportunities. In this transaction, I am making the tragic, difficult decision of exchanging fluency in my native and second languages for a life of success.

Returning

Losing a language (or two), like everything in life, comes with deep regrets. I have experienced contradicting feelings inside me, struggling between what I want and what I must do to succeed in the United States. I unconsciously bought Ilocano and Tagalog books but I have yet to actually open them. These books have proven to be nothing more than a nostalgic collection or a hobby rather than serving as actual language (re)learning tools. In an effort to motivate myself, I am attempting to incorporate Philippine folktales and mythology into my reading list to make my language (re)learning experience more enjoyable. In addition, I also decided to join a local Filipino organization that promotes social interactions with other Filipinos in the area. I guess, in a way, collecting books that capture part of my heritage and becoming closer to other Filipinos in the United States is my attempt to return to my language, culture, and place of origin.

In my life, I often struggle with balancing my authentic Filipino self and the Filipino-American I need to be to succeed in the United States. At the end of the day, I keep reflecting on this never-ending struggle and I wonder, *pagbabalik*[3] "does it even matter?"

Notes

1   The literal translation of the Tagalog word *balikbayan*, *balik* (return) and *bayan* (town), is "return to town". In the Philippines, we use this word to often describe someone returning to their hometown from another country. *Balikbayan* boxes, specifically, are care packages people overseas send to their family and friends in the Philippines. In this context, I am using the term "*balikbayan* boxes" to describe the type of boxes we were carrying.
2   Translation from Spanish: I speak.
3   In Tagalog, pagbabalik means "returning".

Reference

Gide, A. (1973). *The counterfeiters: A novel.* Vintage Books.

CHAPTER 17

My Life's Metamorphosis: Becoming Bilingual

Luis Javier Pentón Herrera

Greatness Starts with Sadness

Every time I think back to my journey of becoming bilingual in the United States, the first emotion I feel is sadness. Arriving in the United States at the age of 16, almost 17, not knowing how to say a word in English was a traumatic experience. Although I was living in Miami, Florida and attending Hialeah Senior High with a large population of Latinx students, being an English learner made me feel unsure of my worth at times. "*Balsero*," or rafter, was a common derogatory term yelled out by bilingual students; not many from the bilingual community wanted to associate with us, English learners. Every time I think back to my time in high school, a feeling of melancholy takes over; I cannot help it.

> Evelyn (classmate) and I were practicing in English the new vocabulary words we had just learned while Mrs. R., our English as a Second Language (ESL) teacher, talked to a colleague. Mrs. R. stopped talking to her colleague and yelled at Evelyn and me, "what are you two doing?!", "Ms., we are practicing English," I shyly replied while Evelyn proudly smiled in agreement. Mrs. R. laughed out loud in front of the class and exclaimed "Yeah right!", giving us a contemptuous look. My heart sank in uneasiness and disappointment; Evelyn's smile withdrew for the remainder of the school year at Mrs. R.'s class.

Most of my memories from high school have faded away; perhaps in an unconscious effort to stop my memory from letting me relive those emotions once again. However, I do remember, vividly, that event at Mrs. R's class; it was the first moment in my life where my inability to speak a language made me feel less than, unworthy, unappreciated, untrustworthy, unwelcomed; *a foreigner*.

Greatness Starts with Self

Because I had completed many graduation requirements in Cuba, my native country, I was allowed to graduate from Hialeah Senior High in just two years.

© KONINKLIJKE BRILL NV, LEIDEN, 2021 | DOI: 10.1163/9789004446182_017

Right after graduation, I joined the United States Marine Corps thinking the little English I had mastered made me an expert; *"ya hablo inglés perfecto"* (I already speak perfect English), I mistakenly used to tell my friends and family so. In hindsight, I believe this idea of being proficient in English was developed in my mind as a result of the pressure and expectations of adults around me. *"Los muchachos aprenden inglés rápido"* (youngsters learn English faster), my dad's friends and neighbors used to assure us often in our conversations. However, as soon as I joined the military I realized how limited my English language was; it was painfully limited.

The first night I arrived at Parris Island, South Carolina (boot camp for the United States Marine Corps), I thought that moment was going to be my last. Drill instructors were yelling left and right, loud screams followed by chaotic and aggressive movements from all recruits. I remember standing at attention on top of those yellow footprints while listening to the cacophony of blasts created by the drill instructors' voices, watching recruits run around and lining up on the yellow footprints and thinking/praying inside my head to my God—whom I call Shangó— *"¡Ay Shangó, mi padre! ¿Qué hago aquí?"* (Shangó, my father! What am I doing here?). I had no idea what the drill instructors were yelling; I was alone, unable to communicate, and shaking in fear that one wrong move could detonate the fury of all the drill instructors there.

The first week of boot camp was the most challenging. As recruits, we were waiting to get "picked up" by a platoon while human resources processed our administrative paperwork. We were not allowed to sleep (short naps only), stand up, or do anything besides sitting down on the floor with our legs crossed. The only phrase I remember from that time is "head call," which I learned meant "restroom break" in military jargon after waiting for a full day to use the restroom because I did not know its meaning. Quickly I learned that to survive, I had to pay close attention to what other recruits did when drill instructors yelled something out. I was disabled—linguistically disabled—but I was not going to let my linguistic challenges take me down without a fight!

During the first few weeks of boot camp, I was able to camouflage my status of English learner by following other recruits' physical responses to our drill instructors' screams. Looking back, I realize I had no idea what was happening most of the time, what our drill instructors were yelling, or why they were yelling. My bunkmate, Recruit P., soon realized that I could not speak (or understand) English very well. At that moment, he communicated with me through gestures and I understood that I needed to keep my eyes on whatever he was doing and replicate his actions. That strategy proved helpful through the first two months of boot camp but, towards the end, the number of our platoon had decreased from 89 to 45 recruits due to the harsh training. At that time, our drill instructors had the opportunity to pay more individualized attention to the fewer recruits still left standing (metaphorically and literally) in our platoon. After my drill instructors discovered I could not speak English very well, the remaining weeks became a living hell. I remember being picked on by my drill instructors for no apparent reason and receiving blame for random things: "it was recruit Pinto bean's fault!"; the drill instructors would yell aloud in the barracks as they joked about my last name. I also remember my drill instructors often telling me to scream the phrase "say hello to my little friend" and would laugh out loud. I was oblivious at what was happening; I later learned that this was a phrase from the renowned movie *Scarface*.

After completing three months of boot camp and almost two months of the infantry training school, I started to notice that my English skills were improving. Full English immersion seemed to be something my brain processed well. I started learning military terms, could blurt out one or two words from the cadence while running, and I could get some of my messages across to my fellow military members and instructors at infantry school, all English-monolinguals or non-Spanish speaking people. I recall thinking to myself, "I don't have to understand everything, just enough keywords to follow along." That strategy certainly proved helpful and carried me all the way through infantry training; I was comfortable with being low key, quiet, and unnoticeable. However, because the universe has a unique sense of humor, comfortability was not in my destiny. After completing my required training from infantry school, I was assigned to Okinawa, Japan, and became a military administrative clerk.

Greatness Starts with Fear

My first memory of Japan was answering a phone call at my new job station, placing the call on hold, walking up to my Lance Corporal (supervisor) and telling him "I don't understand." He saw the frightened, desperate look on my face; nothing more needed to be said. I was not asked to answer the phone again. That night I returned to my room in the barracks, called my best friend, Yanet, and cried out to her telling her "*estoy en una base militar aquí en Japón y no entiendo ni japonés ni inglés, ¿qué hago aquí?*" (I am in a military base here in Japan and I can neither understand Japanese nor English, what am I doing here?). That conversation with my best friend allowed me to release all the emotions that were tightening my chest. It seemed as if each of my tears represented the weight I was letting go; I was depurating my soul. That is the last time in my life I recall ever being fearful of not being able to speak English...to survive, I had to become stronger.

Greatness Starts with Change

With time and the help of amazing military comrades, I quickly learned the ropes of my military occupation. I was physically strong, the fastest in my entire company according to the Combat Fitness Test, and a hard-working Marine. I slowly started to pull my weight around the office. The more I understood English, the faster my fear changed to confidence. The more I opened up and contributed to the office, the more my comrades began to see me as equal. I was no longer the guy who could not speak English, I was becoming the person who could now communicate and take charge in the office. Occasionally, I would experience contemptuous looks (similar to Mrs. R.'s) from officers and high-ranking enlisted personnel who could not believe that I, a person who did not speak English very well, was knowledgeable of my military occupation. For them, my heavy accent and broken English were indicators of my mental abilities and intelligence; they were wrong.

Greatness Starts with Confidence

After honorably completing my military service, now in Virginia, United States, I decided to volunteer at non-profit organizations to explore what I wanted to do with my life. In what I consider a serendipitous event that brought me to a full circle, I was asked to facilitate an ESL class to adult immigrants. My life transformed the night I taught my first ESL class. From that moment on, I knew I wanted to become a teacher and empower immigrants. I still do not know how my English skills transformed overnight; one day I was struggling to write a paragraph, the next day I was pursuing my first master's degree in education with the goal of becoming an ESL teacher.

I like to think that my adult ESL students motivated me...or maybe that my English skills (especially reading and writing) suddenly improved because I had the goal of becoming an ESL teacher. I cannot say for sure. However, one thing I definitely know, I only started to feel like I belonged in the United States the moment I began to gain confidence in my (bilingual) abilities and chose to push my English skills to the next level. I was no longer comfortable feeling low key, quiet, and unnoticeable like I did in the military; I was now beginning to find my voice, my bilingual, confident voice.

Greatness Starts with Hard Work

As a graduate student pursuing my first master's degree in adult education and development, I quickly discovered writing was something I enjoyed doing and, from my professors' perspectives, I did it well. Most of my memories about that graduate education experience take me back to different moments where I was either reading or writing—to this day, I relish those memories. As a graduate student, learning had become such an intoxicating experience that I decided to pursue two additional master's degrees right after graduating from my first. My second and third master's degrees were in Spanish language education and in Bilingual Education and ESL, respectively. Certainly, juggling work and two master's degrees at the same time was challenging, but I felt empowered to keep learning for my students and for myself.

My journey through graduate education was truly emancipatory but it required all the dedication and effort I could muster. I recall using a notebook to create my own dictionary with all the new vocabulary words I was learning in our weekly readings (in English and in Spanish) and studying them every day to integrate them into my own lexicon. Speaking continued to be a challenge for me, especially in front of people but, with dedication, I was noticing how much my writing and reading skills were blossoming. Also, something I had not realized until that moment was that my academic Spanish was not as eloquent as I thought it to be. Certainly, my master of science in Spanish language education pushed me to grow as a critical Spanish writer and reader; I loved the challenge!

My love for education and learning was empowering and intoxicating. For this reason, I decided to pursue my doctoral degree in September 2014, right after I completed my third master's degree. One day, as a doctoral candidate, I suddenly realized that all the struggles I had gone through and all the details I considered flawed about me and my language-learning journey had made me, and my ability to write, unique. While pursuing my Ph.D., I realized that I was one of the very few doctoral candidates in my program who had the skills to write academically-publishable texts in both English and Spanish. I can now understand that my dedication and pursuit for improving my writing in both languages became the passage to my personal and professional empowerment.

Greatness Lives in You

The older I become, the more I reminisce about my experiences of becoming bilingual in the United States. In the beginning, being an English learner was traumatic for me and it produced sadness, self-doubt, and fear—I often felt ostracized, criticized, undervalued, uninvited, untrusted, and/or unwanted. Looking back, I can now see all that time I was feeling down about my English skills I was, in fact, feeling bad about how others perceived me. I was placing more value on what others thought about me based on the way I spoke English than on acknowledging the merits of my own efforts to become proficient. Perhaps I was focusing too much on being accepted, on proving myself and my worth...I felt the need to do so because I saw myself as the foreigner, the one who could not speak the language.

The more English I learned, the less I cared about others' opinions of me. In a way, becoming bilingual gave me a sense of belonging and the power to deal with the occasional contemptuous looks, racist remarks, and discrimination. To this day, I still experience this kind of treatment, even by my own fellow colleagues, I just do not mind it. Instead, as a language and literacy educator, I now focus on what I can do to improve lives and teach two essential skills my students need to succeed in the United States: English and resilience.

It has taken me all this time to come to the realization that becoming bilingual in the United States has been one of the most enriching experiences of my life. It does not matter what anyone ever thought about me, how they treated me, or how they laughed at me. Their actions did not dim my light, did not diminish my intelligence, did not make me any less than what I am. Becoming bilingual was my life's metamorphosis—I spent so much time trying to find perfection without realizing that, all this time, greatness lives within me.

CHAPTER 18

Giving back When Most in Need

Geovanny Vicente Romero

Before moving in 2015 to the United States of America, I had traveled to New York several times to visit family and friends. Yet, the country I would soon call my new home was unrecognizable from the one I had previously visited. As a tourist in New York, it always struck me how many of my fellow Dominicans who had university degrees and professional careers in the Dominican Republic worked full-time as taxi or Uber drivers despite being lawyers, accountants or dentists. Many people from my home country, and other countries from around the world, come to the United States with professional backgrounds but find limited job opportunities, in part because of the language barrier. When I moved to the United States, it took me some time, but I overcame my fear of English and was determined to continue my career in public administration and communications. I gained the necessary experience where I least expected it, through volunteer work, giving back at a time when I found myself most in need.

Volunteering and Job Opportunities

I arrived in Washington, D.C. on May 30, 2015, with a big, new suitcase full of prized possessions and immeasurable hope. I vividly remember riding up the escalator of Washington's Metro Station into my new neighborhood beaming with pride. My girlfriend, now wife, and I were in a state of euphoria because we were finally together, having beaten all odds to make our long-distance relationship become a day-to-day reality. She gave me so much support and enrolled me in an English school during my first week in the country. We spoke Spanish at home, which I now regret as time lost learning English, but that is how we most naturally communicated and understood each other. Despite my classes, outside of the house and in Spanish-speaking enclaves, I felt alone and unable to freely communicate in English. I avoided social gatherings where English would be the dominant language, fearful and ashamed that I could not fully express myself. Certainly, striving for perfection and harboring a fear of failure can be self-defeating, making us our own worst enemy!

© KONINKLIJKE BRILL NV, LEIDEN, 2021 | DOI: 10.1163/9789004446182_018

After taking daily English classes into the summer, I started gaining confidence. For extra practice, I also enrolled in free evening English classes taught by volunteers at a local church in the community. Witnessing how selflessly the volunteers gave their time to teach English inspired me to also give back to my community with one of my most natural skills, teaching Spanish. In my home country, there are limited community and civil society organizations, and thus a less prominent custom of volunteer work. Seeing volunteers in action, with the same dedication, energy, and sense of responsibility that people give toward their professions, inspired me.

While struggling with learning English, I sought comfort in teaching Spanish. After hiding from the world for months because I was ashamed of my English skills, teaching Spanish helped bring me back to my roots. Being able to teach others something I knew well, my native language, helped me practice English more than I could ever have imagined. Many of my students began learning Spanish at a basic level, which required me to speak more English to clearly explain the content in each lesson. Teaching my native language gave me confidence because I saw my own struggles in my students and felt less alone. I saw how my students overcame initial challenges associated with learning a new language, such as pronunciation or grammar errors, and their perseverance inspired me; I knew that if they could overcome those challenges, I could do so, too! The learning and teaching process was humbling and empowering all at once. It was humbling because both I (as a teacher) and my students came to the classroom ready to learn; we were fearless of making mistakes or asking questions in our minds. We understood that mistakes and questions would create deeper learning, which was an empowering experience for me and for students in our class.

I enjoyed sharing my culture with others and helping Americans learn more about the Dominican Republic and understand the differences among people from Spanish-speaking countries. I had been so caught up in my rush to linguistically assimilate to English that I had been blind to the opportunities that Spanish offered me in this new country. History and politics are two of my passions, so I relished the days I got to teach American students thirsty for knowledge about both Spanish and the Latin American region. My students provided excellent feedback to the organization I was volunteering for. My students' feedback made me feel very fulfilled and valued—a void I was looking to fill professionally since I arrived in the United States. It is funny how an outsider's perspective can sometimes help remind us of our greatest strengths.

Going back to our roots and our passions helps make the transition to a new country much smoother. For me, my roots are in the Spanish language and Dominican culture, and my passions are studying history, politics, and communications. I built my Spanish classes to incorporate these topics. Each student selected a country to report on each week in a "press conference" activity that we would do, picking key moments in history to recreate, such as the date marking each country's independence and World War II. At the end of every class semester, we would have a potluck with food and music from each country. I would select the Dominican Republic if my students had not already selected the country, and I relished sharing our talented musicians, gastronomy, and proud moments from our history. American and international students were interested to learn that the Dominican Republic is home to the oldest modern city in the Americas, with the first hospital, church, and university. Santo Domingo, the capital of the Dominican Republic, was where Christopher Columbus landed on his first voyage to the continent.

Soon, my volunteer experience as a Spanish teacher gave way to a paid job as a contractor for the U.S. Government. I taught diplomats, military officials and their family members to speak Spanish before they departed to important posts abroad. Through these day-to-day interactions, I was able to learn a new perspective while earning the respect and friendship of world-class professionals. During our classes, we also discussed cultural norms, distinct language patterns, and slang in the country of their upcoming posting. For example, I shared with students who would be relocated to Peru, that the Spanish word used for "bus" (*guagua*, in Spanish) throughout the Caribbean can get you in trouble if you use it in the same context in Peru. That's because the same word also means "child." I told them how my wife was once traveling in nearby Ecuador and asked someone where she could catch the bus (*¿Dónde puedo coger una guagua?* in Spanish), and the person got very annoyed and walked away. She later found out that the words she used in Ecuador (with the same meaning in Peru) meant, "where can I abuse a child?" Through this painful personal story, my students paid close attention to the correct vocabulary to use and become aware of in the new countries they would soon call home. Fortunately, I did not have an embarrassing moment like this in English, but I wondered, what if I had similar training before moving to the United States? Then, I decided to teach myself the English language the way I taught Spanish to my students.

English Self-Teaching

Learning English can be daunting, but it is absolutely essential to carving out your niche in the United States. I always knew that my dream job in

Washington, D.C. was out there, all I needed to do was perfect my English skills. I began immersing myself more in the language, reading all the books I could get my hands on. As a voracious reader, I devoured all texts I found interesting regardless of genre, including American politics, classic comic books, art history, World War II, and terrorism, to name a few. My wife was amazed at the pace of my reading and comprehension. I understood everything in the books but, in my head, I was translating into my memory in Spanish. Still, I kept a notebook of all the important new words and phrases I learned. Then, I practiced speaking these phrases out loud at home. Once I felt comfortable, I tried using the new vocabulary in daily conversation. The gift of language kept on giving.

As I grew in confidence as an English speaker, I decided to explore new activities and social circles. I made new friends where I could practice my growing English vocabulary. I listened to English podcasts, music, and TV non-stop whenever I was not reading in English—I still do! Studying in English helps me break out of my natural comfort-zone in Spanish. Once I get immersed in English with non-Spanish speakers, even if for a weekend, I get a huge confidence boost. But, if I am not conscious to keep up with my independent learning and keeping in touch with English-speaking friends, I quickly revert back to Spanish—after all, Spanish is my default setting!

Professional Growth

Learning and perfecting a language is a new lifelong journey. The earlier you release your fears and start opening your mouth to practice, the better. Opportunities to serve the community abound in the United States, with some examples including non-governmental organizations (NGOs) like foundations, educational institutions, and support groups. As newcomers to this country, we can explore the amazing community resources available through local and national organizations—a network beyond the public and private sectors that is only just starting to emerge throughout Latin America. Personally, I have been involved with the Global Language Network, UNIDOS US (formerly the National Council de La Raza), Carlos Rosario International Public Charter School, Teatro de la Luna, and the Cathedral of Saint Matthew the Apostle. It is inspiring to see many people volunteering their time to help others and share what they love. As a newcomer to Washington, D.C., I was shy, struggling with English, and needed to contribute to a cause where I could make an impact. So, I got involved with the Global Language Network language club to teach Spanish. Ironically, teaching my native language to Americans, helped me both improve my English and learn more about American culture in ways I could never imagine.

I have since incorporated volunteering into my routine so that I can give back to my community through teaching, environmental cleanup, and as a mentor to young professionals. At the same time, I have been able to continue my career in strategic communications and public policy. I completed a U.S. university master's program at the George Washington University, which has helped me along in this field. I have done public policy and strategic communications consulting work for politicians and international organizations. I have dreams of expanding my communications consultant business and am working on a plan to make this a reality.

So, when it is all said and done, my English is far from perfect, but I have learned to embrace my accent, after all, some people like actress Sofía Vergara make a career out of it! Once you have a base from which to communicate in English, you can add your own *sazón* (seasoning or flavor) and make it authentically yours. I feel I have arrived at this stage now and others can, too. English skills help you empower yourself to follow your dreams in the United States, wherever those dreams may lead. I have also learned to appreciate that our unique cultures and roots make us who we are. While striving so hard to assimilate linguistically in pursuit of success, I rediscovered the value of my native tongue. I stumbled upon this self-knowledge through volunteering and made meaningful relationships with special people during the process. My students and I remain in contact and the learning never stops. Through volunteer work, I also came to terms with the fact that learning is a journey, not a destination. Sure, my default setting is Spanish, but I have made much progress incorporating English into my control panel. To my fellow immigrants, the best advice I can give you is to give back when you feel most in need; it will be one of the best decisions you will ever make in your lives.

CHAPTER 19

Journeying through Transnational Spaces: A Reflexive Account of Praxis and Identity Construction

Rajwan Alshareefy and Cristina Sánchez-Martín

In this chapter, we share our stories of identity formation, negotiation, and tension as we journey through various contexts and cross perceived borders of nation-states, communities, and cultures. Our stories reveal experiences of rebirth, change, transformation, resistance, and hybridity partially enacted in and through language and interaction with our immediate and distant communities. Cristina is a professor at the English Department at Indiana University of Pennsylvania (IUP) and is also Rajwan's dissertation adviser. Rajwan is a doctoral candidate at the Composition and Applied Linguistics program at IUP. The idea of this project came from one of our dissertation progress meetings. We realized that through writing about and reflecting on our experiences with transnationalism, literacy, and identity construction, we become more informed and better equipped to succeed in our journeys. We begin our chapter by presenting our individual narratives, accompanied by evocative images. Rajwan focuses on his transnational identity construction between the United States and Iraq and how political conflicts have impacted his life trajectory and the choices he made. Cristina starts her journey in Salamanca, Spain, where language and gender prejudices dominated her upbringing, leading her to expose these ideologies and push against boundaries and labels of gender, language, and nationality. We finalize this chapter with a reflection of our collaborative narrative process and its impact on our identity construction and praxis as teacher-scholars in the United States.

The Process of Narrating Ourselves: Part 1

Cristina and Rajwan had been discussing transnational and multilingual identities for over a year since Rajwan started to write his dissertation about the discursive identities of international Ph.D. students. In the process of theorizing these identities, it became natural to reflect on our own identities

© KONINKLIJKE BRILL NV, LEIDEN, 2021 | DOI: 10.1163/9789004446182_019

as multilingual migrants in academia. During a dissertation-progress meeting, it became evident that the recent protests in Iraq were impacting Rajwan's research progress. We agreed that such experiences needed to be acknowledged and brought forward in our research and teaching practices. As a response, Cristina suggested that we write about our experiences of border crossing and identity construction in the various spaces we inhabited. We talked about how writing our stories helps us situate ourselves in relation to the work we do and to better understand ourselves. Following this meeting, we set out to write our narratives individually with the goal of putting them into conversation with each other.

Rajwan

It was the summer of 2016 in my hometown, Babylon, Iraq. I was driving home in my father's car and he was sitting next to me. We were talking about my Ph.D. application and the difficulties I was facing in processing my paperwork at the Ministry of Higher Education, then my father said, "لا يظل بالك على وظيفتك (Don't هنا او على اي شي. مو مهم تحافظ على شغلك هنا. اترك هذا البلد وروح حقق حلمك worry about your job or anything here. It doesn't matter if you keep your job or not. Leave this country and go for your dream). I was going to say "what about funding? What about you and my mom? Who is going to take care of you?" Then he continued, "ولا يظل بالك علينا. الله موجود. ركز على مستقبلك ولا ترجع. ما الك مكان هنا بعد" (and don't worry about us. God will help us. Focus on your future and don't come back, there's no place for you here anymore). It was this last statement that struck me the most. Thinking ahead, I visualized myself as a foreigner in the United States, a poorly funded student, and possibly an asylum seeker. I sank in deep silence thinking of the imminent change in my life trajectory. My father was right, it was hard for me, like it was for many others, to survive in post-invasion Iraq where our security was a dream, not a right. Terror was institutionalized and sponsored by corrupt political leaders and government officials whose allegiance is to other countries. It is true that one dream I had was to study abroad and earn a doctoral degree to teach at a university, but in the backstage, there were numerous other reasons and stories that urged me to embark on my journey.

The recent history of foreign intervention in Iraq is one significant factor in shaping the political, social, and economic landscape of the country and eventually its people. One recent and significant example is the United States-led invasion in 2003 and its aftermath. I still remember the day I came back from school in 2005, a few hours after a suicide car bomb attack in the heart of my hometown. The smell and sight of fresh blood and debris, the atmosphere of concern, sorrow, and fear that were consuming the town were excruciating and indescribable. Such atrocities were only the beginning of many waves of violence, assassinations of professionals and scientists, sectarianism, corruption, internal displacement of over four million Iraqis, and countless migrants across the world, to just name a few disasters. Therefore, in a way, my decision to traverse into an unknown future was not entirely a choice.

Figure 19.1 documents the start of my journey back in 2016. In those three suitcases, I packed what I could carry of my belongings. I stepped out of the door leaving behind everything that was dear, bitter, and sweet. On the doorstep, waiting for my ride to the airport, my head spun and felt heavy with all the questions, doubts, and future possibilities. Two days later, I arrived in the United States. My experiences here were as complex as I envisioned them during my conversation with my father. With time, I started to see that, in general, binaries and labels seem to be one dominant way for institutions and communities to identify people and to make sense of the *perceived* social structure. Therefore, at my university, I am an "international student," to the Internal Revenue Service, I am a "(non)resident alien," and to someone else, I may pose a threat by being perceived as a Muslim extremist from the Middle East.

Throughout the past few years in the United States, I came to realize that these labels are by no means accurate or capable of capturing the fluidity and hybridity of my identity. Through socialization with my immediate academic and local communities, I assimilated, negotiated, and resisted cultural practices and norms. Simultaneously, I maintained relations, communicated with, and continued to belong to Iraq. I felt divided between these spaces but did not fully relate to either. "Who am I and where do I fit in?" are the two questions that have haunted me since I arrived in the United States. The answer gets increasingly complicated as the conflict and tension rise between the United States and Iran, two major forces seeking control over resources in Iraq. This U.S.-Iran conflict is being enacted on Iraqi soil. This tension clearly manifests itself in the recent and on-going October protest in Iraq.

In October 2019, an anti-government protest erupted in Iraq over corruption, unemployment, poverty, and lack of basic services. In its attempt to suppress the protest, the puppet government of Iraq killed over 600 and injured over 20,000 protesters. In addition, tens of social activists were kidnapped or assassinated. Iraqi militias supported by Iran have gained immense power over the last 16 years and are now in full control pushing aside the weak government while brutally muzzling patriotic Iraqi voices.

FIGURE 19.1
Rajwan's home, Babylon,
Iraq

Although these events are taking place across the ocean, they are impacting me deeply both socially and personally. My mind is often occupied with the day-to-day stories, news, and developments there. I supported the rebels' quest for a decent life by donating money for the treatment of the injured and following and sharing people's stories, pictures, and news on social media especially during times of total internet and communication shutdown in Iraq. As a supporter of the protest, I was not only endangering my family in Iraq but also running the risk of being accused of serving the "American agenda." False accusation is one of the ways the militias are using to criminalize and terminate young Iraqi protesters and their supporters. At my family's advice, I removed my family name from my Facebook account and hid all of my biographic information from social media to avoid being identified by militias and to save my family from potential retaliation on the basis of my political and patriotic orientations. Recently, a video shared on social media shows members of Saraiya Alsalam, an Iraqi militia, announcing that they have a record of all those who critiqued the Saraiya leader on social media and that they are ready to assassinate them when the time comes. I have critiqued the Saraiya leader in many posts!

With rising political and social tensions, I stand on a shaky ground wondering what my next step would be. On the one hand, settling in the United States can be difficult considering the political discourses against migrants and prejudices fueled by islamophobia, xenophobia, racism, and other ideologies. The workings of these ideologies will continue to (re)shape my life. On the other hand, returning to Iraq does not seem like a viable option I can consider with all the social, economic, and political chaos and the on-going revolution. Living as a transnational individual and realizing my hybridity in a globalized world is costly. My identity will continue to evolve as I respond to the various political and social developments/changes happening across borders and spaces.

Cristina

Imagine a swing hanging on a tree or on a steel and rusty infrastructure. Two long ropes hold the wooden surface on to a branch or the metal frame in the playground, as in Figure 19.2. Knots tie the ropes and the simple piece of wood all together as one single infrastructure where I situate myself.

Do you imagine the swing moving back and forth? Or, on the contrary, does it remain static? I see the space created by the swing from one side to the other and even perhaps going in circles as a transnational space, an expansive symbolic place beyond static identities, languages, and territories.

I have come to realize that my transnational experiences resemble those moments of sitting on a swing and, with that movement, I remain located and harnessed through the knots that tie the swing, creating space to understand, identify, and possibly transcend identities that through the years might have seemed immutable.

Let's go back to the swing I introduced at the beginning of my narrative. The swing represents my transnational identities. Even though it is located in a specific place, I create, by expanding through the movements of the swing,

FIGURE 19.2   Columpios/swings
PHOTOGRAPH BY ESTANISLAO BARRIO MONTES

an alternative symbolic space beyond and despite the knots that hold the swing itself. The knots that hold me in the swing are factors that mediate and sometimes constrain my identity construction. These knots illustrate the contradictions between my experiences in movement and the static factors such as institutional regulations and discourses around my identity that prevent certain aspects of my identity to change.

Because I have learned to identify, appreciate, and understand my identity as dynamic, I have found more space for growth, which I continue to nurture. As a multilingual woman in the United States academic context, I carry with me previous trajectories, including my language repertoire and gendered identities. In fact, one of my most salient identity traits, and perhaps, the first type of mobility I noticed was language. Early on, since I was a child, I pushed for the swing to move as I strived to understand the concept of language. These early attempts at creating space were fun opportunities for self-inquiry.

I grew up in Salamanca, a small city in the Northwest of Spain. During the week, I attended school in the city, but most weekends and during the summertime, my family (my sister, my mom, and my dad) and I would visit my grandparents and relatives in a small farming village 45 minutes away from Salamanca and whose playground is depicted in the picture at the beginning of this narrative. In school, I learned to conjugate and memorize correct language forms in Spanish, and examples of language deviations associated with perceived lower classes, especially from rural communities, were often ridiculed. At the same time, conversations at the dinner table in Salamanca revolved around *accurately* learning certain words in English, French, or Catalan (what my mom had learned as a teenager working as a waitress under exploitative conditions). However, in our farming village, rule-free and creative language practice was only frowned upon occasionally by outsiders-*forasteros*. This dissonance between language accuracy and creativity quickly sparked my interest and I embarked on a project to keep a record of my grandma's and her friend's language practices, which, to me, seemed like a rebellious act against the rule-governed and snobby language expectations I was being schooled into. By observing and writing down conversations between my grandma and other elderly women in the small farming town, I learned the value of their expanding and creative ways to communicate, despite existing prejudices around them.

Years later, after a study abroad program at Durham University in the United Kingdom, I realized these kinds of linguistic prejudices were far more common than I had imagined. These prejudices permeated all societies, impacting most vulnerable populations, usually middle and low socio-economic classes, migrants, and women; conditions that could all intersect at once. Soon after returning home, I read Gloria Anzaldúa's *Borderlands/ La Frontera* about hybrid language identities marginalized for their incapability to fit into established categories and groups of speakers. In particular, the sentence "I am my language. Until I can take pride in my language, I cannot take pride in myself" (1987, p. 81) deeply resonated with me, not just for her call for language justice but because of the gendered dimensions of language ideologies. Yildiz explains that the phrase "the mother tongue" is connected to monolingual and prescriptivist language views: "The 'mother tongue' is the affective knot at the center of the monolingual paradigm and therefore a knot worth unraveling" (2012, p. 10). The "mother tongue" is, for Yildiz, a language romance, created from a positivist and masculinist mindset, despite appearing to honor women's motherly identities. Therefore, prescriptivist approaches to language, like the ones used to ridicule my grandma, emerged out of territorialized and monolingual discourses connected to the mother tongue, which in return, continue to exist to control language behavior, learning, and opportunities for personal growth.

I am back in the swing, pushing against these limiting ideologies but recognizing their existence. I move back and forth in the swing, little by little pushing a bit further and creating more space. I have been able to identify, occasionally pushed, and even transcended the boundaries that discourses around language and gender had imposed on me. The metaphor of the swing affords me dual points of reference, that rather than being opposed to each other, define themselves through the movement. As a teacher-scholar, I now strive for my students to find their own metaphors for transnational identities and practices in ways that contribute to their self-realization. At the same time, I continue to learn from them as well as from the women across the world to continue to language in creative ways, to push the boundaries of what is recognized as valuable, to be heard, and ultimately, take ownership of their own lives.

The Process of Narrating Ourselves: Part 2

After finishing and exchanging our narratives, it struck us that, despite writing about our transnational selves, our experiences seemed to be hard to reconcile. Therefore, we decided to come together and discuss where our stories met. Cristina's realization of her privilege as compared to Rajwan's description of the atrocities of war and its aftermath became a topic of conversation and contention; while Cristina was emphasizing our differences based on privilege, Rajwan continued to bring back attention to what made us both individuals with transnational identities and orientation. Two themes of similarity became part of the conversation: (1) despite how his experiences of survival had shaped his identity, Rajwan's perceived accented English had some impact on his claimed and assigned identities in the United States; (2) Cristina's realization of her participation in protests against the invasion of Iraq in 2003 indicated that, besides language difference, her transnational identity was built on an awareness of world-wide conflict and how uneven political power and actions shape people's daily lives. These themes of similarity, framed from an acknowledgment of our different individual lived experiences, help us conceptualize transnational identity construction and account for it in our own endeavors. First, we believe that, as educators, we must move beyond the connotations emerging from labels such as "international multilingual" students or teachers. In fact, our narratives reflect dissatisfaction with labels as well as our ongoing efforts to carve out space outside of assigned identity markers.

Therefore, we must account for the divergent experiences of our students that oftentimes emerge, directly or indirectly, in our writing or language courses. In fact, offering opportunities for other students to narrate their lives through language, visuals, and collaborative narrative writing projects enables reflection on our trajectories by juxtaposing them with others at the intersections of privilege and marginalization. In our case, Cristina can better understand her privileges against Rajwan's positionalities and lived experiences. This collaborative reflective practice makes evident the factors that mediate our mentoring, and thus, it can help us identify possibilities to transcend the barriers imposed by outside forces.

References

Anzaldúa, G. (1987). *Borderlands/La frontera: The new mestiza.* Aunt Lute Books.

Yildiz, Y. (2012). *Beyond the mother tongue: The postmonolingual condition.* Fordham University Press.

CHAPTER 20

Story Weaving: Tejidos de Conocimientos Que Nos Conectan al Territorio

Judith Landeros

Stories are like rebozos, weaved tightly, each tejido embodying conocimientos of our histories that connect us to our ancestors and territorios. I was first introduced to the concept of stories by my amá.[1] These stories served as tejidos that trespassed colonial borders connecting me from Cicero, IL, USA to Michoacán, México, the Land where my mom and maternal ancestors are from. As a child, I began to notice that my mother's stories varied in their method of delivery. Some stories felt urgent while others invited me into a world of imagination. Sometimes these stories were quick dichos and I learned about the multiple meanings words can carry. Other stories were shared visually like when I observed my mom prepare masa and transform it into tortillas, gorditas, or huaraches. My favorite stories were the ones that introduced me to my mom's way of life in el campo, the games that she played as a child, and all the things she would do as the eldest sister to help care for her siblings. Many of these stories were shared with me when my mother and I were actively engaged in planting, cooking, and conjuring nourishing food with our hands.

Carrying Our Stories, Migrating with Our Medicine

"We are people who carry our medicine, our plants, everywhere we go." Maestra Marika, a Lipan Mescalero Apache elder and Medicine Woman in Austin, TX shared these words with a group of us, her students. Her words inspired me to engage in the practice of story weaving and create digital illustrations to visually represent my mother's storytelling. These stories and illustrations embody the ways that migration, food, plant medicine, and language intersect across landscapes. In the sections below, I draw from a digital story weaving approach to honor my amá's relationship with plants, the water, the Land. These stories have taught me about where I come from as well as positioned me to ask: what are the stories of the people that are stewards of the Land I currently live on? What are the native plants to these Lands? How have they been impacted by the imposition of colonial borders, displacement, and English language policies? I share these visual illustrations with the hope that as a reader you will respect them and seek to learn more about your relationship with the territory you live in, the territories where your ancestors come from, and your relationship to the environment and more-than-human kin.

Bolsitas de chiles y yerbas

Our pantry in Cicero, IL was always full of dried chiles and different medicinal herbs. I remember bringing back dried chiles and yerbas when we would drive back to Chicago after visiting our grandparents in México. I would help my mom hide the bolsitas de chiles y yerbas between our clothes in our suitcases so that when we arrived in Laredo, TX, the immigration patrol officers would not give us any trouble at the immigration customs checkpoint. My grandma would always send my mom a small package of the medicinal herbs and chiles with my uncles whenever they would visit. These medicinal herbs helped heal me whenever I had a cold or empacho.

FIGURE 20.1   Bolsitas

Judith: Mami, ¿que te mandó mi abuelita con mi tío?
amá: Son unos chiles de árbol y unas yerbas.
Judith: ¿Y lo dejaron pasar en el avión? ¿Te acuerdas cuando regresamos de México y en la frontera nos dijeron que no podíamos pasar las plantas?

amá: Si, yo creo que escondió las bolsitas entre su ropa, así como hici-
mos nosotros la siguiente vez que regresamos de México.

Tortillas en el fogón

I remember standing on a chair next to my mom making little tortillas while
she made the bigger ones that we were going to eat with our dinner. She would
tell me to keep practicing so that my tortillas would come out round and not
chuecas. Once I was a bit older, she would let me flip the tortillas on the comal
con mi mano. Amá would tell me how she would wake up every morning before
sunrise to molder el maíz and make masa for the tortillas. As the eldest of her
fourteen siblings, she was responsible for making tortillas for the family. She
explained to me that before they got a gas stove, she would make the tortillas
en el fogón which they would use wood to start the fire so that the comal could
heat up.

FIGURE 20.2   Tortillas en el fogón

amá: Todos los días me levantaba bien temprano. Molía el maíz y hacía
el nixtamal.
Judith: ¿Qué es nixtamal?

amá: Es lo que se usa para hacer la masa. Se le pone cal. Y luego me ponía a tortear en el fogón de la cocina de tu abuelita. Hacía unas pilas de tortillas para que todos los tragones comieran.

Corundas en el cerro

I grew up eating corundas which are a traditional type of tamales from the state of Michoacán, México that are wrapped in cornfield leaves. At first, my mom would also bring the hojas de milpa from the rancho and freeze them back in Cicero, IL to preserve them. When we did not go to México as often, my mom would plant corn in our backyard during the summer and we would use those leaves to make the corundas. My mom always made a caldillo (soup) and a special salsa that was served with the corundas. Corundas were always my favorite and I loved listening to my mom tell me stories of how she would eat corundas and go to the cerro and eat them with her family.

FIGURE 20.3   Corundas

Judith: Mami, ¿Quién te enseñó a hacer corundas?
amá: Me ponía a hacerlas con mi mamá Agustina y nos íbamos al cerro a comer corundas con la bola de chiquillos para que se pusieran a chirotear y no dieran lata. Y cuando íbamos de regreso, la abuela

Agustina me decía que pelara el ojo para recolectar yerbas como gordolobo, cola de caballo, y aceitilla para hacer remedios.

El ojo de agua

My mother is a water carrier. Many of my mom's stories revolve around collecting water from the waterhole in the rancho where she grew up. She would go to el ojo de agua to get water to bring back to the house for cooking, drinking, showering, and watering plants. Sometimes she would carry a tinaco on one arm and other times she would grab a stick to put on her back and tie two buckets on each end. Mom has always taught me to not desperdiciar el agua.

FIGURE 20.4   El ojo de agua

amá: Yo me iba al ojo de agua a acarrear agua para tener para cocinar y tomar.

Judith: ¿Y como le hacías amá?

amá: Me ponía un palo en los hombros y dos botes a los lados y así cargaba el agua. Mi papá Agustín me decía que parecía hormiga.

Story Weaving: Disrupting the Hidden Curriculum

In my kindergarten to twelfth grade schooling experiences, these cuentos and ways of knowing, or conocimientos, became the supplemental curriculum that I did not receive in my bilingual classroom. Although I benefited from a transitional bilingual program from kindergarten to fourth grade, I was taught in Spanish with the long-term goal that my literacy skills in Spanish would transfer to English and I would no longer need a bilingual education. The transitional bilingual program created a space where I could continue to learn in Spanish, but simultaneously served as a tool to conceal the hidden curriculum that upheld whitestream values and omitted histories that would expose Spanish as a colonial language. Even when I was taught in Spanish, the textbooks narrated the history of the United States from the perspective of white settlers and rarely included people from my culture and background. At school I was not taught to interrogate the creation of borders, or the criminalization and xenophobia towards immigrants. In school, no one mentioned the history of the Spanish language in Latin America and that there are various Indigenous languages that are still spoken there. My amá's stories, without me fully being conscious of it in my youth, kept me from assimilating and actually ignited a passion to learn more about where I come from.

It became evident when I started my career as a bilingual teacher of young children that the plantita literacy and food literacy I knew was predominantly only in Spanish because it was intergenerational knowledge passed down from my mother. These literacies were not legitimized or affirmed in my schooling experiences from Kinder to my Master's degree, but I would find myself bringing those stories and conocimientos into my classroom when I taught preschool and first grade students. With preschool students I co-created a unit with the help of parents and community members about the environment. One of the activities involved students creating their remedios book based on the knowledge parents and community members shared with students. As a bilingual teacher, I did not have many curricular resources in Spanish. Most of the curriculum in Spanish was directly translated from English to Spanish that centered whitestream values and was not relevant to my students' lives. This awareness led me to create my own curriculum guided by the stories my mother had shared with me. I integrated the stories that my students, their families, and community members already carried with them (González et al., 2006; Yosso, 2005). I recall seeing the excitement of my young students as they were able to recognize a plant that they had seen at home, a smell that they smelled in their kitchen, or would share about the traditional foods they would eat at home. Plantita literacy and food literacy have the potential to unfold the hidden curriculum in schools because they create generative connections to language, culture, identity, migration, medicine, healing, storytelling, and relationships to Land, the environment, and more-than-human kin.

The memorias, vivencias, and teachings that my mother generously gifted me with are medicine to the soul that have profoundly impacted my identity and teaching praxis. I was born far away from the territory where my ancestors are from. However, my mother's cuentos, her memories, and the plant medicine and traditional food that has nourished me since I was in her womb remind me that mi cuerpo es mi primer territorio and that I am connected to the territorio where my amá, abuelita, bisabuela, and tatarabuelas come from.

Note

1   In this chapter, I use the word "amá" to refer to my mamá (in Spanish) or mom.

References

González, N., Moll, L. C., & Amanti, C. (Eds.). (2006). *Funds of knowledge: Theorizing practices in households, communities, and classrooms.* Routledge.

Yosso, T. J. (2005). Whose culture has capital? A critical race theory discussion of community cultural wealth. *Race Ethnicity and Education, 8*(1), 69–91.

CHAPTER 21

Entre la Tierra y los Sueños

Pablo Montes

We do not inherit the land from our ancestors, we borrow it from our children.

NATIVE AMERICAN PROVERB

∴

La tierra nunca se olvida

My parents, like many of those who are forced to migrate, made the journey at their youth in search of a life that seemed more promising than what our little ranchito (ranch) back in México could provide. With little money, no documents, and having only a few years of formal education, they embarked on a journey towards the United States. Although they lacked material aspects, they were guided by a vision, the power to dream, and the land that would always wait for their return. Leaving the land which has been home for many generations prior, one can only imagine the pain that comes with this separation. Because we are of the land, the land will always await our return. But, at their youth, my parents knew that their journey must be made elsewhere. They understood the risk of not being able to return and, as resilient as they could be, it pained them to know this truth. One day, however, they would return. With them, their own family, and the lessons that come with our continued migrations. These lessons are to teach us why returning to our ancestral homelands was not just a journey back home, but a journey towards a return to us.

La memoria en la[1] agua

Although my dad eventually received residency because of the Amnesty Act of 1986, my mom lived undocumented until 1994 where she was finally able to complete paperwork to gain residency. This meant that my parents had to drive from Wisconsin to Ciudad Juárez, México in order to appear in front

© KONINKLIJKE BRILL NV, LEIDEN, 2021 | DOI: 10.1163/9789004446182_021

of an immigration attorney to approve all of my mom's documentation. In the middle of February1994, they started their drive towards El Paso, TX and shortly after passing St. Louis a hose burst in the car near the city of Rolla, MO. It was late in the evening, which meant that there were no auto shops open so they could make any type of repairs. With nowhere to go, they spent the night in that little car in the coldest month of the Midwest. Curled up all together were both my parents and my older sister who was three at the time, and by this time my mom knew that she was pregnant with me. My dad kept turning off and on the car to provide a little bit of heat without overheating the engine, and so they went the night till the morning came. That morning they were able to fix their car and continue towards the desert heat of New Mexico and West Texas. My mom tells me "tenía tanta sed…Y no había ninguna gasolinera y ya casi se nos acababa el gas…creo que por eso te gusta tanto la agua" (I was so thirsty…And there were no gas stations around and we were almost out of gas…I think that is why you like water so much). A few days in El Paso and they finally had their meeting in Ciudad Juárez where my mom was finally granted residency. With no hesitation, they made their way back to Guanajuato to reunite once more with the lands that have always been home. A feeling I can only imagine—to feel free to move; to make a return back home knowing that it will not be the last, but one of many; to make these migrations ancestral journeys. Growing up, people wondered why I would drink water with almost anything I ate. I now know. Esa agua tiene memoria (that water remembers). I drink because my body remembers those maternal waters that cared for me amidst her thirst. I drink to honor that which my mom could not have.

Entre el deseo y un derecho a soñar

After my younger sister was born, my parents decided to permanently move to México. However, we ended up in Wisconsin so I asked why my parents ultimately decided to move back to the United States after all. In México, we had begun a business of selling rotisserie chickens out of our home and many people from our rancho would buy from us. "¿Y por qué se fueron si estaban ganando bien?" (And why did you leave if you were earning good money?) I asked my dad, and he responded "Uno de momento es lo que uno quiere pa' uno…no pa' ustedes. Es muy diferente decidir por uno, por lo que uno quiere…lo que uno está viviendo en su momento…y no piensa uno en ustedes hijo. ¿Qué es lo mejor para ustedes?" (For a moment, that is what one wants for oneself. Not for you all. It is very different to only decide for oneself, for what one wants. For what one is living in the moment. And one doesn't think about you, son. What *is* the best for them?" For a short period of time, that is what we want for ourselves, not for you. It is very different to have to only decide for oneself.

Although my parents wished to stay in México, to make a life in the land that gave so many of our generations an opportunity to grow and live, together they came to the realization that to stay meant to leave a dream behind; that to desire for only oneself came at a sacrifice to others. As much as their desire urged them to remain, the land gave them solace that one day, when the time came, this journey would lead them back home carrying the fruits of our dreams that could have only been cultivated elsewhere. So, with selfless love, my parents sold everything they had from their business and collected all the money that they had saved from selling rotisserie chickens to make their final, and permanent, move back as humbled guests to the lands of the Ho-Chunk and Potawatomi people, or better known as Wisconsin. Since all my siblings and I had been born in the U.S., there were few legal roadblocks upon our move. However, emotionally, I know my parents decided on not staying home to carry home elsewhere for us. What I have come to learn from this lesson is that there is a difference between living just for one's desire and living for a right to dream together. Now with all of my siblings moving to Texas, I know that it is our time…for my siblings and I…to dream for the life my parents now envision. For our parents, their lives' dreams mean going back to nuestro rancho (our ranch). To take care of the land that has patiently waited, so that one day, when my siblings and I return, we are met with our dreams of all those years, the dreams that were dreamt before, and the dreams that are yet to come.

Una educación que la escuela no te enseña

For many years while permanently living in Beloit, WI, we made the yearly journey back to our rancho de La Luz, Guanajuato. Oftentimes, we would leave for about six weeks during the months of December and January. Due to our extended stay in México, every year the schools would denote our absences as truant and would often try and charge us for "excessive truancy." Our academics often suffered too since losing six weeks of class instruction was always seen as impeding our academic success. At the time, I agreed with what my teachers and other educators would say; that losing class instruction was an academic divestment. Many teachers were not always accommodating and, back then, I blamed my parents for my poor grades. I believed, like many others, that grades and objective ways to determine knowledge were representative of all that there is to know. I saw my parents, with little formal education, as people with no education, with no theories, and with no philosophies of life. In this sense, the education system was working—to miseducate me on the legacies of my people.

It was not until years later that I realized what my parents were doing; providing me una educación (an education) that no school could ever teach me. I see educación not as a mere translation of education, but una educación as a cosmology of life and a theory passed down by generations of knowledge. My parents were able to cross half the continent of North America by remembering how they did so years before. How to navigate multiple worlds and create their own systems of communication. They instilled in my siblings and me the importance of paying homage to the land where our ancestors lay whether it be for three days or six weeks. In addition, my parents also taught us why this return home was much deeper than a simple vacation. Our migrations reflect our journeys of strife, resilience, and hope. This type of education, schools can only imagine providing. My parents were my first teachers, the best researchers I have come to know, and the manifestation of the brilliance that has come before us.

La tierra no se vende, se ama y se defiende

As I continue forward through my life, all I can feel is honor and humility knowing that I come from generations of knowledge keepers. Through our yearly migrations, I was able to learn more about my family's history. Part of this history was knowing that among the people in our rancho, our family is one of the oldest families to live there. Which means that, for many generations, there has been a parcel of land that has been passed down through my family. One of my parent's wishes is to never sell the land. La tierra no se vende (the land is not for sale). The reason why, he says, is "porque esa tierra nos ha dado de comer para vivir. Esa tierra es de la familia. Es parte de nosotros" (because this land has fed us. This land is of our family. It is part of us). To come back in a full circle, I know that our migrations have meant so much more than just a culmination of separate journeys. Each travel to our lands provided guidance and lessons to learn and they continue to do so. I share a part of my family's migration stories because they are the knowledge that has stayed with me for all these years. I cannot think of selling the land, a relative that has taken care of my family and continues to gift us the prickly pears that grow in our yard, the flowers that bloom on our grandma's patio, the tortillas that we prepare from the corn we harvest, and the well where we get our water. Those lands hold the memories, dreams, and life of my ancestors and the future generations to come. Those are the lands that welcome us home every year. Those are the lands, that for as long as our family may walk this earth, will be protected by us. Because we are of the land; that is both a lesson and a teaching.

Note

1   In our rancho, and within our diction, we use "la agua" instead of "el agua"

CHAPTER 22

The Power of Digital Storytelling for English Language Education: A Reflective Essay

Polina Vinogradova

Several years ago, a student in my *Technology for Language Teaching and Learning* course gave me a very personal and touching gift—a digital story. She produced this digital story as a project for the class, but it was not yet another unit plan or paper that we (professors) generally assign in our master's Teaching English to Speakers of Other Languages (TESOL) courses. It was a short multimodal narrative in which the author, my student, expressed who she was, showed what mattered to her in her life, and what her great passion and interest was. She was a musician, a talented pianist passionate about piano music, who, following her parents' direction, did not pursue music as a career. If we had not done a digital storytelling project in our class, probably, I would have never known this about her, I would have never received a gift that touched me deeply.

Digital storytelling has been a part of my professional explorations for the past 15 years. It started with my fascination with and appreciation for purposeful multimodal meaning-making. This meaning-making affords space for the author to create a powerful message by carefully composing, selecting, and combining visual, verbal, and musical components into a powerful personal narrative. A digital story itself is short, but in three to five minutes, a powerful multimodal story develops (Lambert, 2013; Vinogradova, 2014). And within each component, multiple layers of modalities and meaning can be present, making the narrative even more powerful.

A New Way of Self-Expression

For a dyslexic bilingual who at that time viewed herself as a non-native English speaker, digital storytelling presented a new way of self-expression. One might ask, why this differentiation between a bilingual and a non-native English speaker is important. Let me explain. I started learning English as a foreign language (EFL) as a subject in second grade when I was eight. English was a part of my schooling and professional life since then. I received an undergraduate

© KONINKLIJKE BRILL NV, LEIDEN, 2021 | DOI: 10.1163/9789004446182_022

degree in English language education and taught EFL at a university in Russia before coming to the United States to pursue a master's degree in TESOL. And while I have been living in English and with English as one of my two languages, I saw myself as a non-native speaker of English. This concept implies a position of deficit. Instead of emphasizing that I comfortably live and work in two languages (and English has been my primary language for almost 20 years), I was focusing on who I was not (as in not a native speaker of English), rather than on who I was—a person who fluently and comfortably functions in two languages. And the latter means being bilingual.

To me—a dyslexic person positioning herself as a non-native English speaker (a double deficit)—multimodality of digital stories offered an opportunity to be creative in various ways. I could produce my own content as well as repurpose creative multimodal material that was already out there—family photos, existing videos, drawings, music, chunks of text, to name a few. It was about going beyond just words and writing, and finding and using forms of expression that, instead of reminding me of my limitations and shortcomings, could help my voice to get out there. It was ultimately about empowerment, about dismissing the deficit approach to creating and narrating, about dismissing a deficit approach to language learning.

When I think about digital storytelling, the impact it made on me, and the potential impact I saw it could make in language education, I think about Sarah Shin's (2007) article, "For Immigrant Students, the ESOL [English for Speakers of Other Languages] Glass is Half-full." As she wrote this article in *Essential Teacher* thirteen years ago, this idea of viewing English language learners from an asset perspective does not seem to be ground-breaking any longer, which is encouraging. But as I work with English language teachers and TESOL candidates, I often hear the conversations of what the students will not be able to do rather than what they would, could, or could potentially be challenged to do. The focus on what is possible can empower us to experiment and see what type of learning and engagement might happen. This experimentation informs teaching and learning innovation. And many teachers are interested and eager to experiment with multimodal assignments and projects. But they are constrained by strict curricular guidelines and expectations, standardized assessments, an administration that might not have the flexibility or necessary vision to create room for this experimentation, lack of resources, perceptions of parents, and perceptions and expectations of the learners themselves. The more I worked with digital storytelling, the more I started seeing this genre as a way to challenge, reformat, and to a certain degree flip our preconceived notions of what 'good' language teaching and learning means.

Letters from the Gnome

Ever since I can remember, I struggled with writing and reading. For a child growing up in Leningrad, Soviet Union, in the late 1970s–early 1980s, there was an expectation to know the alphabet and be able to read and perhaps write in block letters by the age of five. This was not happening to me. I remember enjoying listening to records with fairy tales and children's plays and leafing through thick books looking at colorful illustrations, but I could not read. I knew the letters, but putting them together to elicit the meaning was laborious and took away the pleasure of reading. When I was close to six, I still could not write, which was quite devastating to my highly educated and ambitious parents who put great value on literature and intellectual pursuits.

One morning, a cardboard mailbox with my name on it appeared next to the entrance door in our apartment. In it, I found a letter from a Gnome addressed to me. It was short and written in block letters with some drawings, and I was thrilled to read it and eager to respond. I remember spending hours trying to write a reply with a brief introduction, but some letters and words were just not cooperating with me. This correspondence with the Gnome continued for quite a while, probably for more than a year. The letters were a combination of text, drawings, and various small craft projects, and multiple colors were involved. Gradually, the letters from the Gnome started to become more 'serious' as my pen pal started using cursive, and drawings and pictures were disappearing giving room to more cursive text. Reading those letters in cursive, I started to suspect that the Gnome was my mother, and with that realization and increased amount of reading and writing necessary to respond, I started to lose interest. The cursive aspect is important here as it was a mandatory part of 'good' writing in Russian. It had to be tidy and clear and was expected to become a part of one's uniqueness as a writer. You would also be judged on the quality of your cursive writing.

I do not remember how the Gnome project ended; it seemed to have faded away. But I vividly remember the next level of struggle with reading and writing when I started elementary school. By then, I could read and write, though I never enjoyed it and saw it as very hard work. I could recite quite a few poems and children's stories and was considered to be adequately prepared for school. But I just could not do well on writing assignments, tests, and spelling dictations. I would write a sentence in one word, miss letters, flip syllables, and write wrong vowels. When reading, I had to sound out every single word in my head in order to put the meaning together. I still read like this, which takes a lot of time and a lot of mental work. This level of struggle with the written word has been a constant presence in my life. I was never assessed or diagnosed as dyslexic. It was not something that was done in schools in those days. The realization that perhaps my struggles had something to do with dyslexia came much later in life.

Experimenting with Digital Stories

I came to the United States to continue my graduate study and was pursuing a master's degree in TESOL. In an introductory linguistics class, we were exploring brain processing and disorders associated with language learning. I wrote a paper on dyslexia and hyperlexia and was fascinated and amazed that I could now have an informed explanation of my reading and writing experiences. I was not a bad student, a bad writer, and a bad learner anymore. I was dealing, coping, and finding ways to work through a learning disorder and doing it quite successfully, I must say. And I was in an educational setting that privileged and required high levels of literacy and constant engagement with and production of the written word.

In recent years, there have been a number of articles in the media written on the topic of dyslexia (e.g., Curnow, 2019). Curnow's piece particularly spoke to me as it actually narrated the story of my life. She wrote about the struggles with "spelling tests, rote learning, reading aloud in class and standardized tests" (para. 8)—all of my enemies at every step of my schooling. She cleverly showed how she, a dyslexic herself, would be misspelling multiple words in her own writing: "Then there's the speling (spelling). In fact, just having to spell "dyslexic" is a constant frustruation (frustration). As I've been writing this I've spelt it "dylesic" "dyslexic" and "dsyleix" (Curnow, 2019, para. 6). In excitement, I forwarded the article to a friend and immediately misspelled "dyslexic."

One might ask, why I am writing about my dyslexia in the context of digital storytelling, and specifically in the context of using digital stories in English language education and my work with English language learners and teachers. To me, this sets the stage and explains my interest and excitement about a genre that emphasizes multimodal meaning-making and creativity. By no means I am equating learning an additional language with a learning disability (even though there are still educational institutions that house English language programs under the umbrella of learning disorders). But there are some overlaps in the types of struggle that we experience as people with learning disabilities and people learning another language. And I have experience with both.

English language learners, especially the ones learning English as a second language (ESL) in English-medium settings, the ones with lower levels of literacy and English language proficiency, experience limitations and constraints in communication on a regular basis. Communication in class becomes yet another reminder of what English language learners cannot do or do not know; communication outside of class reminds of these limitations again, at a different level, and often is accompanied by mistreatment and discrimination. And even if the motivation to learn the language is high and you know how important it is to you and your family, constantly struggling and moving against the tide is exhausting and frustrating. As a dyslexic English language learner and a language teacher, I was looking for ways to change this dynamic of deficit and constant focus on what the students do not know. And let me just point out here that before I started this search, I had taught for a number of years following this deficit perspective, not seeing my students' glass as half-full, but rather focusing on what was missing. By the time I was introduced to digital storytelling and started exploring the work of Joe Lambert and his colleagues at the StoryCenter,[1] I was looking for a different approach and different pedagogy that could build on students' interests, their knowledge of life, and their rich experiences. I was looking for a pedagogy that could facilitate the creation of a community where it is not just about learning the four language skills, doing homework, practicing new grammar, and reading and retelling stories and conversations that might not be particularly relevant to the students' lives. I was looking to incorporate culturally responsive pedagogy—a pedagogy that "highlights the interplay between identity, language, and learning" (Thomas & Carvajal-Regidor, 2021) that Thomas and Carvajal-Regidor so compellingly describe as sustaining, revitalizing, caring, and participatory. I was also looking to create room for multimodal materials and forms of expression in the ESL curriculum as I was becoming fascinated by the work of Kress and van Leeuwen (2001) on multimodality and the New London Group (2000) on a pedagogy of multiliteracies. This led me to design a *New Media and Culture Course* for intermediate university ESL students and collaborate with colleagues in integrating digital storytelling and a pedagogy of multiliteracies in several content-based ESL courses that focused on intercultural communication, academic life, and development of academic English language skills.

I have written before about my work in this area, using digital storytelling projects with university-level ESL students in the U.S. (see Vinogradova, 2014; Vinogradova, Linville, & Bickel, 2011). This work informed and inspired my current use of digital stories with TESOL candidates.

Over the years, I have incorporated digital stories as projects in my *Technology for Language Teaching and Learning* course. I invited TESOL candidates to produce digital stories on the topics important to them.[2] More recently, follow-ing a student's suggestion, I have been asking TESOL candidates to transform their teaching philosophies into digital stories (see Figures 22.1 and 22.2 for examples).

FIGURE 22.1   A frame from a digital story (digital teaching philosophy) by Mariana Grassi (MA TESOL, American University)

FIGURE 22.2   A frame from the digital story (digital teaching philosophy) by Melissa Krut (MA TESOL, American University)

It has been a fascinating learning experience for me. Fascinating in several ways. I see TESOL candidates experimenting with digital multimodal compos-ing and finding various ways to engage with multimodality. Some question the flexibility of the project, wondering whether what they are doing is what I am expecting them to do. Others are concerned about the technology aspect of the project and whether they have enough skills and knowledge to carry out the work. Some students wonder how this can work in their teaching. They

assess resources, collaborate, give each other feedback, offer help, and ultimately engage in continuous critical reflection in this process. And this reflection is not only about the project itself, it is also about pedagogy.

In their collaborative work, conversations in class, and reflective writing, the
students regularly analyze and refer to their own learning, think about their
teaching, and consider learning that can happen for their students. Several
TESOL candidates pointed out to me that this project puts them in their students' shoes, it reminds them of uncertainty and struggles ESL learners can
experience, it shows them how scaffolding, collaboration, and creativity in the
classroom can facilitate a supportive community of practice.

I want to point out here that the first time I asked my TESOL candidates
to transform their teaching philosophies into digital stories, it did not work
out as well as I had hoped. I discovered that I had not thought through some
nuances and details of the assignment, did not offer enough guidance, and did
not clearly show how the students could connect their digital stories with the
reflective paper I asked them to write. This was another illustration to me of
how well thought through and pedagogically sound a project like this needs
to be.

All these are significant aspects of critical digital storytelling that prompt
English language learners and teachers to engage in critical reflection and
assessment, evaluate our own knowledge, and identify the type of support
and resources we need to implement digital storytelling projects. This critical
reflection also prompts the students to assess what they need to produce digital stories that they want to produce.

This brings me to the beginning of this essay, to the gift I received from my
TESOL student. This brings me to thinking and reflecting on how much I have
learned about my students, their interests, and their lives. This also gets me
thinking of how much I have learned about teaching and about myself as a
dyslexic language learner and language educator. Perhaps that is why digital
storytelling became such a defining genre in my academic and teaching career.
Every time I think about digital stories produced by my students, every time
I get an email from a former student telling me how they have used digital
stories with their own students, I get excited and inspired even more.

Notes

1   See https://www.storycenter.org/
2   For an example of a TESOL candidate's digital story, go to https://vimeo.com/265269480

References

Curnow, R. (2019, June 6). The upside of dyslexia, even as a journalist. *CNN Health.* https://www.cnn.com/2019/06/06/health/dyslexia-benefit-curnow/index.html

Kress, G., & van Leeuwen, T. (2001). *Multimodal discourse: The modes and media of contemporary communication.* Oxford University Press.

Lambert, J. (2013). *Digital storytelling: Capturing lives, creating community* (4th ed.). Routledge.

New London Group. (2000). A pedagogy of multiliteracies designing social futures. In B. Cope & M. Kalantzis (Eds.), *Multiliteracies: Literacy learning and the design of social futures* (pp. 9–37). Routledge.

Shin, S. J. (2007). For immigrant students, the ESOL glass is half-full. *Essential Teacher, 4*(4), 17–19.

Thomas, M., & Carvajal-Regidor, M. (2021). Culturally responsive pedagogy in TESOL. In P. Vinogradova & J. K. Shin (Eds.), *Contemporary foundations for teaching English as an additional language: Pedagogical approaches and classroom applications* (pp. 90–99). Routledge.

Vinogradova, P. (2014, July). Digital stories in a language classroom: Engaging students through meaningful multimodal projects. *The FLTMAG.* http://fltmag.com/digital-stories

Vinogradova, P., Linville, H. L., & Bickel, B. (2011). "Listen to my story and you will know me": Digital stories as student-centered collaborative projects. *TESOL Journal, 2*(2), 173–202.

CHAPTER 23

Lost and Found: A Story of Reclaiming Identities

Bashar Al Hariri and Fatmeh Alalawneh

Unrealistic expectations of life in the United States have, for years, fooled immigrants with dreams of a "new beginning." Specifically, for many immigrants and individuals living abroad, Hollywood's representation is the closest reference they have of life in the United States. Unaware of the complexity of education, healthcare, social, and economic layers, some immigrants arrive with a preconceived notion that starting a life in the U.S. is as easy and simple as they see in the movies. However, many are shocked when they find themselves perceived as "the other" in a community that, in many cases, challenges their cultural and social identities. Being part of the society and culture of *the other* mostly implies isolation and lack of acceptance from the mainstream society. Immigrants, thereafter, navigate their daily lives in shock and woe. Nevertheless, they are determined, no matter what, to work on their goals and build a brighter future for themselves and their offspring.

We, Fatmeh and Bashar, are a couple who arrived in the U.S. from Jordan where we met. Bashar, originally from Syria, met Fatmeh back in Jordan, while we were both attending graduate school at Yarmouk University. Bashar migrated to Jordan after escaping from Syria because of the war. After completing our master's degrees in Jordan, we wanted to move to a new country to seek better opportunities for ourselves. We decided to apply to U.S. universities to continue our education, to succeed, and to live our American dreams.

After the long process of collecting and filing papers, we landed at John F. Kennedy International Airport in New York with similar dreams and expectations, which we had watched in movies and TV shows for years. All we were seeking was love, acceptance, new beginnings, and walking down the street in Manhattan. After staying for a couple of days in New York, we had to report to campus at a private university in the Midwest.

When we arrived at that university, we, along with our cat (Kiki), were oblivious of the people around us. Shopping at Walmart, which was the only store in that small town, did not make us think that our lives there would ever be the same again. After visiting the office of international students at our university, we started to look for apartments to rent. The quest to find a new apartment was not easy. We were both surprised to learn that the town did not have public transportation and we were even told by university employees, "why do you need a bus when you can have your own car and go anywhere you want. This is freedom; this is America!". We both did not think much beyond that sentence and we were very happy to hear the word "freedom," which we both longed for many years. After five years in the U.S., we are no longer the same couple that landed in New York; the journey we have embarked on has transformed our identities and beliefs. In this chapter, we depict our experiences as international students and hopeful immigrants in the United States.

Introducing Diversity

Bashar

I am a tall guy, 6.1 feet to be exact. When I arrived in the U.S. I learned that guys like me are called "big guys" here. In addition to being tall, I also have a distinctive Middle Eastern look. What most people know of Arabs and Middle Easterners is the Hollywood portrait of long beards and frowny, angry faces. People were not able to see me as a cheerful, funny guy who enjoys jokes and sharing Syrian food with friends and strangers. Instead, they could only see me through the Hollywood lens, and I was not given a chance to show who I truly was.

I am a speaker of both Arabic and Russian and learned English as a third language. One of my first memories in the U.S. was of feeling shocked and horrified when a couple, who were driving their car near my university, suddenly stopped and screamed at me that I was not welcome in this country and offended me with racial slurs. I did not know what to do. I sat down on the sidewalk and called my wife, Fatmeh. When she answered the phone, I was not sure what to say and all that came to my mind was that I did not want her to be uncomfortable and worried when I left the house alone. This incident happened a couple of times when I was by myself, yet it never happened when I was with my wife. One night, I opened my laptop and searched on Google to learn what immigrants do when they are in a similar situation. Thinking back, I think I was trying to recreate the idea of having a (virtual) support group. After lots of readings and talking to people who had been in my shoes, I learned about diversity and how diversity is becoming an issue of concern for many politicians, researchers, scholars, and even communities as a whole here in the United States. I also learned that different universities, states, and cities are trying to diversify their campuses and communities to truly represent the essence and core values on which this country was founded upon. After months of reading many books about diversity, my life has never been the same.

Fatmeh

I was born in Romania to a Jordanian father and a Romanian mother. Although I am a Jordanian girl, I mostly look European. For this reason, I believe I have been treated differently on and off-campus in the United States. After Bashar's incidents, I started to pay more attention to how people react when he is present, and how we made some people feel uncomfortable because of how Bashar looks. I started to live in a conflict where both Bashar and I wanted to be part of society, we wanted to belong to our new community, and we wanted to be accepted in our new home, but some people prejudged us as bad neighbors. My university professors were very supportive; they were great mentors who encouraged, guided, and supported me in my first semester. Being a female from the Middle East, I was always taught to be silent and not to speak my mind. Because of those reasons, I left the Middle East. I chose this time in the U.S. to speak up about diversity on campus and among my colleagues and international students. It seems that diversity and multiculturalism are sensitive topics on university campuses and not many people are interested in bringing it up. For this reason, Bashar and I decided to transfer to another institution where we would be accepted and appreciated for who we are.

Bashar and I started to become aware that how we look matters. We began to read more about diversity and even drove to other university campuses to attend multiple training sessions about inclusion and social justice. We both decided that a move to a more diverse city was a necessity and so we did. We were both awarded teaching assistantships at a state university in the Midwest and hoped for a better start to our graduate experiences.

Self Acceptance

Bashar

I was accepted at a state university as a teaching assistant to pursue a master's in English as a second language (ESL). In any typical graduate ESL class, students talk about their teaching experiences, teaching philosophies, and the noteworthy incidents they observed in their ESL classrooms. Among the noteworthy incidents shared in one of my master's classes was the preconceived idea that, if an English learner (EL) wants to learn English, they should only be taught by native speakers. This preconceived idea also brought up the issue of speaking English with an accent. I was amazed to hear about my peers' stories. I was judged many times in the United States because of my English accent. I was even told many times, "how come you are doing a master's degree and do not know how to pronounce correctly?". I, of course, attribute this to the lack of diversity and exposure some individuals have to different cultures. However, I was empowered by my classmates' stories and how we are all being judged based on how we speak and how we look. These discussions made me more motivated to promote tolerance and celebrate cultural differences. As a result, I became more involved with the Office of Diversity and Inclusion at my university to arrange events where we celebrate diversity and multiculturalism in our campus. At these events, we deliver the message through formal presentations that we have a lot of commonalities despite genders, identities, colors, accents, languages, and whatever excuse people might come up with to divide us. Consequently, through this journey, I also began to accept myself again and embrace my identity as opposed to how I used to feel before, often thinking that I needed to change myself to be relatable.

Fatmeh

I was accepted in the same program and at the same university as Bashar. In our program, we became known as the famous couple studying the same degree. Part of my assistantship was to teach composition classes to international students. Some of the international students were not content with having a non-native speaker teaching them composition and English, especially in a U.S. university. My students made me very self-conscious of my accent; therefore, I decided to buy accent reduction books so I would sound *American*. I cannot deny that I had an identity conflict because of my English accent and that I wanted to be American, sound American, and eat American. I wanted to do everything as American as possible so that I might acquire the American accent. During that time, I started to attend teaching English to speakers of other languages (TESOL) conferences around the country where I met and talked to many scholars and professors who have been in the field for over 30 years. I attended many of their keynote presentations and was empowered by the discussion I had with them individually on this matter. All these incidents made me accept my English accent and made me recognize that as long as I am speaking grammatically correct and mutually intelligible English, my accent does not matter. My professors also empowered me to accept my accent and my identity. At the same time, I was introduced to the concept of World Englishes where more than one version of English exists.

The two years Bashar and I spent pursuing our master's degrees transformed us. Our beliefs evolved from feeling ashamed that our English was not American to realizing that diversity is power, and it is what makes this country great. We did not let those who doubted us because of our accent and our identity deviate us from achieving our goals. Graduating from the ESL program made us very aware of the stereotypes drawn on ELs. This awareness made us

more resilient to refute those behaviors, to call for social justice, and to promote a more tolerant mindset among students on campus.

English with an Accent

Bashar

I was not aware that many people off or on-campus care so much about the
way I, and other immigrants, speak. When I used to work at a grocery store,
one of my coworkers told me, "it is unpatriotic to not speak American English."
I found it pointless to start a conversation with him about it, so, instead,
I printed out an article for him about "World Englishes." This article (Ishaque,
2018) also shares the important fact that English is spoken and taught by
non-native speakers more so than by native speakers around the world. I, of
course, made a note at the top of the article telling my coworker, "I love the U.S.
(with my accent) as much as you do."

When I was hired as a Visiting Assistant Professor at the same university
I graduated from, I realized this new position was empowering many international and immigrant students who had attended my composition and linguistics classes. Many of them asked me "How come you do not care about the way
you pronounce words?" Those students also asked me if I fake an American
accent when I present at conferences or in college meetings. Besides my
long response explaining why accents do not matter, I reminded them that
Americans themselves speak different dialects and there are many countries
around the world with English speakers who do not speak American English.
I learned later that my students began to support each other when confronted
by individuals who would criticize and judge them based on their English
accents on campus. This has made me proud of my students' resilience and
I continue to work tirelessly with the Office of Diversity and Inclusion and
the Office of Multicultural Success to resolve these issues which hinder immigrants and international students' success.

In addition to working at my university campus, I have also begun partner-
ships in our community. Recently, I started to offer short presentations at non-
profit organizations in my community where I teach and help refugees and
immigrants navigate their daily lives and support their family members. I share
with them that our identities, differences, and accents make this country great.

Fatmeh

My European appearance has made some people deem me an American
who can be talked to "safely." However, the moment people would hear me

speaking with an accent, they would start to ask all kinds of questions. I was very annoyed by this behavior, so I decided to be myself and refused any judgments or assumptions. I started to attend identity and diversity-related conferences where my interaction with attendees and their different stories empowered me to reclaim my identity. I became a member of different committees, which seek to empower ELs and help them succeed in the United States. When I graduated from the master's in ESL program, I applied to a Ph.D. program in curriculum and instruction at the same university. I was awarded a Graduate Dean's Fellowship, which focuses on promoting diversity, access, equity, and inclusion at the university.

As a Fellow, my main objective is to observe and suggest to the Dean of Graduate Studies what can be implemented to help diversify the campus and promote students' inclusion regardless of their backgrounds. Through the fellowship, I met many international students who talked about their identities and how being in the U.S. has forced them to become Americanized because they fear that no one will understand their cultures. This is where I step in and hold casual meetings with them to talk about how we can approach these topics and how the university can be more welcoming and inclusive toward them, so they would not feel alienated or left behind. I am very humbled by the experiences I hear from all students on campus and what strategies they have followed to survive their own identity crises. I also volunteer at a non-profit organization, which supports adult immigrants to pursue their education. I also teach ESL to refugee women who want to go back to school and seek a better life for their families and themselves. I feel very happy every time I am able to provide resources and guidance to adult students. I remember how difficult it was for me when I arrived in the U.S. and found little aid until I figured things out by myself. These students' resilience inspires me to push myself further and to go out to help other ELs. I also want them to be aware of what is waiting for them on the other end and provide them with all the support and guidance they might need along the way.

Currently, Bashar and I are working at different organizations, both of which aid adult and immigrant ELs pursue higher education. We teach ESL classes to immigrants and refugees and do our best to share our experiences and the difficult time we had to overcome when there was no one to guide us. In our work, we remember to tell immigrants that they are part of this country, we all are, and that wherever they go, they contribute culturally and linguistically to this nation. As ESL teachers, we both believe that it is crucial to teach ELs to be confident and to not be embarrassed by their accents. Accents make them unique and it is part of their identities, which they should be proud of. In our classes, Bashar and I focus on diversity by creating our own narratives and by adopting different non-mainstream curricula. In addition, we do our best to always include our students' cultures in our teaching. Bashar and I had a difficult start in the U.S., but by keeping an open mind, staying flexible, and embracing our true selves, we got to where we are today. Today, we are living our American dreams, proudly, with an accent.

Reference

Ishaque, R. K. M. (2018). Empowering English speakers through diversification and promotion of world Englishes. *Advances in Language and Literary Studies, 9*(6), 93–100.

CHAPTER 24

The Weight of a Name: My Names and Stories across Lands and Time

Tairan Qiu

> *"I want this one! Wait, no, go back!"*
> *"This one?"* asked Mama.
> *"Yeah, the one with me standing on the playground,"* I responded.
> *"You sure? This is your last chance,"* Mama said, *"I'm going to bring them to the copying shop tomorrow and scan them so you can get these digitally."*

Mama and I were going through old photos. As we flipped through the pictures, we reminisced about our immigration and migration experiences captured in each frame. These frames pulled us into a tornado of memories about our triumphs, joys, griefs, sorrows, and challenges. In this chapter, I invite you to flip through some of these pictures with me and relive the beautiful memories that the photos elicit.

The aforementioned conversation is also a glimpse into the countless hours I spend talking to my parents using WeChat, a telecommunication social media tool used by most people in Mainland China. Being 13,442 miles away from my parents, the pixels on screens and decibels from microphones are the only things keeping us connected. But it was not always like this.

Life as 邱泰然 (Qiu-Tai-Ran)

Summer 1999, What Does My Name Mean?

I remember it was a hot summer day in Kunming, Yunnan, China. Mama, Baba, and I were walking to the market to buy groceries for dinner.

"我的名字是什么意思?" (What does my name mean?) I asked.

"邱是你的姓, 泰是你们这辈人的字辈," Baba said, "你出生的时候你爷爷给你起的邱泰冉, 代表冉冉升起, 因为你是早上八点多出生的。" (*Qiu* is your last name, and everyone in your generation in the Qiu family has *Tai* as their second character. When you were born, your grandpa gave you the name of *Qiu-Tai-Ran* (冉), representing rising up steadily, because you were born around eight in the morning.)

© KONINKLIJKE BRILL NV, LEIDEN, 2021 | DOI: 10.1163/9789004446182_024

FIGURE 24.1   Pride on my face after learning the meaning of *Tai-Ran*

"后来我们把你的名字改成了邱泰然," Mama added, "我们想让你事事泰然
处之。" (Later, we changed it to Qiu-Tai-Ran (然), we want you to face your difficulties like "泰然处之.")

Being six years old, I did not know that "泰然处之" (Pronounced Tai-Ran-
Chu-Zhi) means *solving difficulties with ease*, but I knew it was something
positive. Years later, I learned about the infamous Chinese proverb "泰然处之"
in school. Mrs. Qing, my elementary language arts teacher, explained to us that
it is a traditional proverb that comes from literature from the Dong Jin Dynasty
(317-420 B.C.). It means dealing with difficulties with ease and grace, and being
natural and calm. I was the most popular kid in class that day. In my journal,
I wrote: "I have a really cool name."

Summer 2001, Last Day as 邱泰然

In the international terminal of our small local airport, my family and friends
came to see us one last time, before we left for Canada. They told us to take
good care of ourselves. They said we could always come back if life got too hard
across the ocean.

Mama sat me down, "然然, 我跟你大妈商量了要给你选个英文名字, 最后我
们选了Terry。去到那边你就要叫Terry了。" (Ranran, I consulted with your aunt
about what English name to give you, we ended up with Terry. After we get
there, you are going to be Terry.) Terry. T-air-rie. I had to learn how to pronounce my new name "correctly." Mama and Baba told me that I needed an

FIGURE 24.2   Family seeing Mama, Baba, and me off at the airport

English name so my new Canadian classmates could pronounce it. I had to be called Terry so I could fit in and so I would not get bullied. Terry, that was my new tag. 14 hours later, I started life as Terry.

Life as Terry Qiu

Fall 2001, Wearing Red?

Our first home in Canada was Toronto. I had to be in the English as a Second Language room for most of the day, but I made a friend in my "regular" class who knew how to speak Mandarin. She translated a lot for me and taught me the "right" things to do in school. She told me to not stand up when answering my teacher's questions—I was used to standing up because I was trained to do so in China. She wrote down the lyrics of the Canadian National Anthem for me so I could sing along during school assemblies. She also taught me the pronunciation of some of my classmates' names.

I also got into our school choir a few weeks after I started school in this new city. The day before a performance, our teacher must have told everyone to wear red tops. However, I did not get the memo—I wore pink that day, several shades lighter than my peers' outfits. My teacher had to find a red vest from a big black plastic bag for me. Seeing Figure 24.3, I was not reminded of how well my first "show" went. Instead, I was reminded of the fear and embarrassment that I felt when realizing that I wore the wrong top. Life as Terry was not off to a good start.

FIGURE 24.3   Choir performance in pink

Winter 2001, My First Christmas

My parents left their university professor jobs in Kunming so they could give me a better education and a brighter future by moving to an English-speaking country. As new immigrants in Canada, they had to build a brand-new life from scratch. My Baba hopped between jobs such as packing fruits in grocery stores, working on the assembly line in shampoo factories, loading trucks for clothing companies, and tutoring rich kids. I vividly remember watching him walk down the dark hallway of our 35-level, old apartment building in his heavy brown coat, leaving for work. He would always leave in the evening and come back home early in the morning.

When my first Christmas came around, I wanted a Barbie doll, like all little girls at that age. "泰然, Barbie 要不别要了, 明年再给你买," Mama said, "我们带你去mall逛逛吧!" (Tairan, let's not want a Barbie, we'll get it for you next year. We'll bring you to the mall and walk around!) We went to the Eaton Center and Mama and Baba got me a red stocking from the 99-cent store. I also got a picture with Santa (Figure 24.4). I felt like the happiest kid, celebrating my first real western Christmas.

Spring 2002, Starting over in Vancouver

Five months after landing in Toronto, we relocated to Vancouver, Canada because there is a larger Chinese community there and the weather is similar to our hometown – Kunming; at least this was how my parents explained it to

FIGURE 24.4   Picture with Santa

FIGURE 24.5   Swimming with Baba in a lake

me. You see, Kunming is famous for its warm weather all year long, and it is called the Spring City. Unlike Toronto's freezing temperature for almost half of a year, on average, Vancouver is much warmer.

In Vancouver, Mama and Baba found manual labor-intensive jobs in a clothing factory. Mama also worked at Little Caesars Pizza. We rented the basement of their co-worker's house—we lived in a house! Baba made delicious food for us like stir-fried rice noodles and garlic and chili tripe. I stayed home alone during the holidays because Mama and Baba had to work. We rode the bus to Stanley Park and lakes (Figure 24.5) and beaches on weekends. We celebrated birthdays, milestones, Chinese New Year, and Christmas. We had family jokes and favorite restaurants. I had endless books from the local public library to read and I made some great friends. I spoke Kunmingnese at home and English at school. Mama always made me recite Chinese poems and practice the multiplication table. I started getting used to my life as Terry and started to love it.

Spring 2004, Last Day of School

Figure 24.6, shows my last day of 4th grade at Renfrew School, also my last day of school in Canada. I did not look excited, even though I was at my favorite spot. I said goodbye to my teachers and principal. My friends and I sat together for one last time in the gym for the Morning Assembly. After the Assembly, Mama scolded me because I had mostly Cs on my report card from an office called the Vancouver School Board.

Also, Mama told me that we were moving back to Kunming.

"Moving back to Kunming? What do you mean? Can I get *Mary Kate and Ashley Olson's* books in Kunming? Where am I going to go to school? You know I am not going to go back if I cannot go back to my old elementary class, right? Where are we going to live? Is our apartment going to have stairs like where we live now? I don't even remember how to write my name in Chinese anymore. Why? Why? Why?" These were some of the many questions I asked Mama and Baba on our walk home that day. They comforted me and said: "You'll be okay. After all, your name is 泰然 (dealing with challenges with grace and ease), right?"

FIGURE 24.6   The playground and report card

Life Back as 邱泰然

Summer 2004, Who Am I

Beijing was our first stop before arriving in Kunming. Baba took me to the Forbidden City to see where ancient emperors lived. He gave me 10 Yuan to buy ice cream while he smoked outside. I remember practicing in Mandarin multiple times before going up to the uncle[11] behind the counter.

"请给我一个冰激凌!" (Please give me an ice cream!) I said.
"好的! 你要什么味道的?" (Okay, what flavor do you want?) he asked.
Shoot, I did not practice this part. I want vanilla. I don't know how to say vanilla in Chinese, I thought to myself.
"嗯…能给我白色的那种吗?" (Um...can I have the white kind?)
"白色? 你说的是香草?" (White? You mean vanilla?) he replied.
I nodded.

FIGURE 24.7   First stop, the forbidden city

I did not know what "香草" (vanilla) was but all I wanted to do was go find Baba. Luckily, I got vanilla. I was happy I got the flavor of ice cream I wanted but I had no idea what was waiting for me ahead.

As 邱泰然 again, switching my dominant language of communication back to Chinese and experiencing reverse culture shock made me very confused about who I was for a long time. My cousins and classmates told me that I was just a banana—yellow on the outside and white on the inside—person and I was not Chinese. They told me I should not feel good about myself because

I had good English. They told me I should go back to Canada and be a 洋鬼子 (Yang Gui Zi, a Chinese slang for [mostly Caucasian] foreigners, derived from the long colonial history in China, often used as a deprecating insult). I just wanted to be a normal kid like everyone else, but I was not. To them, I was the other. To myself, I was neither.

Life as Tairan Qiu

Fall 2011, Leaving Town Alone
After middle school and high school in Kunming, Mama, Baba, and I made the tough decision for me to come to the U.S. for college education. This time, I was alone—two continents and one ocean away from the land, people, and food that I knew and loved. I made the intentional decision to use Tairan Qiu as my name. This time around, I did not want a new tag so others can pronounce my name.

FIGURE 24.8
Family seeing me off at the airport

Spring 2012, College Life as an International Student

"She's still young, her English is good, she'll adapt quickly," people said.
"You're the one who made the choice to go to America, deal with it," some said.
"You can video-chat with your family, stop complaining," others said.

FIGURE 24.9   First college class in the U.S.

Yes, my English was "good," but just my daily, conversational English—what about the English I needed to navigate my studies in a completely different educational and linguistic system? Yes, I made new friends—but can I make new parents, new aunts, new cousins, and old friends? Yes, I can cook my own Chinese food—but what about the oily chilly and rice noodles that my grandma makes that I dream about? Yes, I can video-chat with everyone I love in China—but what about my friends' helping hands or joking laughs when I trip and fall? And what about my Mama waking up in the middle of the nights to pull my kicked-off blankets back on me?

In classes, I could not make my nerves up to speak up because I was afraid of making mistakes. I could go a whole week without any social interactions except for going to class. I could not figure out how my classmates knew exactly when quizzes were because I was not aware of the existence of syllabi. I could spend a whole day reading the same chapter to make sure I understood every word and sentence in my 300-page textbook. I could not go grocery shopping with Mama and Baba. I could precisely find my home in Kunming using Google Maps. I could do a lot of things, but the *could nots* were more than the 17-year-old me could undertake.

I was shook. I was culturally shook, linguistically shook, and academically shook.

Spring *2013, Tuna Melt Sandwich*
"*Bang, bang, bang, bang.*"

During my junior year, gunshots broke the silence of my harmonious university campus. Immediately after the incident, students, faculty, and staff received university-wide texts and emails to shelter in place.

FIGURE 24.10
The leftover tuna melt sandwich

It's probably just one of those false alarms, I thought to myself, as I warmed up my tuna melt sandwich (Figure 24.10). My friends blew up our WeChat group, talking about the text that we received from school.

> Him: *Is everyone safe?*
> Her: *Yeah dude. It seems so real this time!!!*
> They: 大家注意安全啊啊啊 (Everyone be safe ahahah)
> Me: *Calm down guys, it's okay.*

"Bang, bang, bang." I would never forget those knocks on my door. As I opened it, I was greeted by three police officers. I could not remember a lot after that. However, I remember blue and red lights surrounding our apartment, packing up books that I needed for school as quickly as I could, shaky ice-cold hands, shivers and goosebumps, an unfinished sandwich, and a strong yearn for safety. I ran away from my home-away-from-home, feeling everything but calm.

I hustled towards my boyfriend's (now husband) classroom building because he was the safest person I could think of at that moment. My friends kept sending updates in our group. A picture popped up—a guy in a police van. I zoomed in. I looked closer. That's when everything made sense.

That night, I was scared to watch TV, but I knew ever since I saw that picture. The shooter was my roommate, Cody, a person that I shared the same kitchen, bathroom, and living room with. I was the last person he saw before he took the life of another student with multiple gunshots and even more knife stabs. Fear, insomnia, doubt, random interview requests on Facebook, police station visits, confusion...the complementary package of a shooting incident that we see on TV and in movies fell into my lap, without me asking for it. I definitely did not 泰然处之 (solve difficulties with grace and ease).

Spring 2017, Joy

Years later, I had graduated from college and completed my master's program in Gainesville, Florida. I was accepted to the Ph.D. program that I wanted, my boyfriend and I were finally going to end our long-distance relationship, and my parents were in the U.S. visiting me. That moment standing on Wall Street in New York City (Figure 24.11), I felt fearless and proud.

FIGURE 24.11   Graduation trip to NYC with Mama and Baba

As Tairan Qiu, I built a life for myself in this country that was once foreign to me. Even though snapshots of darkness were still crisp and clear, I lingered more on moments of joy. I recalled the few good conversations that I had with Cody, and I think of him as a person with too many stories to tell but not enough listeners. I remembered long phone calls with my parents and the hugs that Mama and Baba gave me when I went back to China during summers. I thought about the strong friendships that I have built. I felt the hug my supervisor at work gave me after telling me to "reclaim my power and be in control" of my life. I remembered my English professor who I respect dearly telling me to stop making excuses for myself. I remember the strength I felt when I passed my master's thesis defense. I remembered that my name, Tairan, means dealing with difficulties with ease, grace, and resilience.

Life as Mrs. Tairan Qiu

Summer 2019, Keeping My Last Name
Before marriage, my partner and I went through long conversations about name-changing. Women taking their husbands' last name after marriage is not a tradition in my culture, but it is a tradition in his. My last name, Qiu, accompanied me as I lived my life as 泰然, Terry, and Tairan. It represents my culture, homelands, histories, family lineage, and legacy of resilience.

FIGURE 24.12   Hair tying ceremony on our wedding day

The past is never static or truly complete because present-day experiences can mediate the past, with its own characteristics, shapes, misfortunes, discoveries, and epiphanies. I am becoming a better interpreter and teller of my stories as I live my life in the process of negotiating my histories, presents, and futures. My name represents the past that lives and grows within me. My name carries the weight of my stories across lands and time and my intersectional lived experiences. I kept my name, 邱泰然/Tairan Qiu.

What Is in a Name?

With migration across geographic locations, immigrants are most often compelled to assimilate to the dominant culture in order to survive. However, it is time for us to reconsider our ways of being. One way to do that is to ask, *What is in a name?* I challenge you to ask this question about your name or other peoples' names. I urge you to learn, explore, and embrace histories and cultures that live within different names. If you cannot pronounce someone else's name, learn it. If others cannot pronounce your name, teach them. A name bears more weight than we realize.

Note

1   In Chinese culture, we generally address elder men as "uncle," rather than their names.

Printed in the United States
By Bookmasters